Henry Newton Dickson

Meteorology

The elements of weather and climate

Henry Newton Dickson

Meteorology
The elements of weather and climate

ISBN/EAN: 9783337275983

Printed in Europe, USA, Canada, Australia, Japan

Cover: Foto ©Andreas Hilbeck / pixelio.de

More available books at **www.hansebooks.com**

The Elements of Weather and Climate

BY

H. N. DICKSON

F.R.S.E., F.R.MET.SOC.

Methuen & Co.

18 BURY STREET, LONDON, W.C.

1893

CONTENTS

PREFACE

—

In the earlier stages of the study of meteorological science, the student has in most cases the advantage of familiarity with the general nature of the phenomena he has to consider. I have endeavoured in this book to utilise this common knowledge, and to show the methods of eliminating its errors, and of arranging it in scientific order. An attempt is thus made to lay down a certain amount of " permanent way," specially adapted to practical purposes, but at the same time leading towards the more theoretical grounds of modern research.

For the benefit of those who wish to pursue any branch of the subject farther, numerous references are given in foot-notes. Since this book was written, the results of recent work in Germany have been presented in elementary form to English readers by Professor Frank Waldo in his " Modern Meteorology," to which the non-mathematical reader, who is interested in the theory of the subject, is referred. Like other departments of physical science,

meteorology does, however, steadily tend to become in-
debted to the higher mathematics ; and its development can
be best studied, failing the original papers, from Professor
Abbe's collection of translations, recently published by the
Smithsonian Institution.

My best thanks are due to Dr. Hugh Robert Mill,
Librarian to the Royal Geographical Society, and to Mr.
R. S. Cole, R. N. E. College, Devonport, for friendly help
in revising the proofs.

H. N. D.

Oxford, *September*, 1893.

METEOROLOGY

CHAPTER I.

FUNDAMENTAL FACTS.

1. *Weather.*—The word weather is ordinarily used to denote (or, rather, connote) the general condition of the atmosphere at any particular time, and especially of the thin layer of it near the surface of the earth which more immediately concerns us. Thus the word is commonly coupled with such adjectives as "good" and "bad," which are strengthened or not according to the effects produced upon us or our interests individually. But weather may be good or bad in a great variety of ways. A very rainy day is not "good," although it be dead calm ; neither is a rainless day on which there is great wind ; and worst of all, perhaps, is one with neither rain nor wind, but a still, dank mugginess, or a raw, penetrating mist.

2. *Elements of Weather.*—Such variations suggest that weather is a general result produced by the combined action of several different elements, each consisting of a special set of phenomena in the physics of the atmosphere, such as those depending on its motion, warmth, transparency, or the like. We are accordingly led by a process of induction to analyse weather into various constituents, the study of each of which forms a separate branch of meteorology.

3. *Meteorology.*—Meteorology is the name given to the science which deals with the physical conditions and

A

changes of the atmosphere generally, whether directly concerned with weather or not ; and its ultimate object is to account for atmospheric phenomena by considering the earth as an astronomical body revolving round the sun as a source of heat and rotating on its own axis, and then deductively to predict them from such considerations. It will be our business to inquire first what are the beliefs about the weather suggested by everyday experience, how far those beliefs are untrustworthy and why, and in what direction more reliable information is to be sought. We shall in this way be led to rediscover for ourselves some of the leading principles of modern scientific meteorology, and to make use of their practical applications.

4. *Sources of Information.*—To begin, then, with the results of everyday experience of the weather, we must first ascertain from what sources our facts are to be derived, and then examine the nature of the evidence. There can be no doubt that the best experience is the most dearly bought, and we may therefore look for it amongst those who have most to gain or lose from accurate observations of the weather, such as, for example, farmers, sailors, or fishermen. Again, it will be admitted that those beliefs are most worthy of examination which gain the concurrence of the largest number of competent judges. Hence we select those most commonly accepted as accurate, and in this there is, fortunately, little difficulty, for we find everywhere a current weather folk-lore, formulated in the shape of sayings and proverbs, which may fairly be taken to represent general experience, and discussed accordingly.

5. *Prognostics.*—The proposition laid down in a weather "saying" or proverb is usually to the effect that if one event happens, a second is to be regarded as probable ; the probability of the second event succeeding the first being deemed sufficiently great to justify an observer of the latter *forecasting* or predicting the other. The chance that if the

first event happens the second will follow it is expressed in the usual way, as the ratio of the number of times the second event follows the first to the total number of times the first occurs. Take, for example, the Scotch proverb :—

> " A wet May and a winnie,
> Makes a fou stacky and a finnie."

This means that out of a large number of cases in which the month of May has been wet and windy, the majority have been followed by an abundant harvest, and that therefore such a harvest is likely to follow any particular wet and windy May. The value of this saying as a prognostic is simply the ratio of the two numbers ; thus, if out of 50 wet and windy Mays all are recorded as having been followed by good harvests, the prediction for any one season would almost amount to a certainty ; if 33 good harvests were recorded, the odds would be about 2 to 1 in favour of a successful prediction ; while if we had 25 good years, the chances would be even and the prognostication worthless. Or, generally, if we denote "certainty" by 1, the chance of any event happening again which has already been known to happen a times out of n is $\frac{a}{n}$, and the chance against its happening is $\frac{n-a}{n}$.

It may be said that as yet all weather forecasting depends on the principle just explained. The aim of the meteorologist is, of course, to obtain a knowledge of the chain of causes and effects connecting the first event with the second, and in that way to be able to demonstrate that, given the first event, the second *must* happen, whether it ever happened before or not. The changes of the weather, although not " uncertain," are nevertheless extremely complex, and a deductive method of forecasting is still in the distant future. In the meantime, we adhere to the old method of " probabilities," trusting to a better selection of "first events" for more successful prediction of the second.

6. *Causes of Error.*—This leads us to inquire what are the causes of error which make certain weather prognostics so much less accurate than others. The first is obviously to be looked for amongst *errors of observation*. Observational errors are of two kinds, personal errors depending on individual peculiarities, and errors common to all observers. With the first class we are not at present concerned, since we are dealing with results obtained by many observers, whose personal errors may be assumed to neutralise each other. But such an assumption cannot be made about the second class of errors, since the probability is not that they will counteract each other, but that they will be all in one direction. By way of illustration, suppose an iron plate placed on a table and allowed to remain until it is known to be neither hotter nor colder than the air. If two people try to estimate the temperature of the plate by touching it, they are more likely than not to form different impressions. Again, let the same people try to estimate the temperature of the plate by touch after it has been immersed in boiling water for a time ; in this case the impressions will also probably differ, and we observe that the individual who thought the plate coldest before now thinks it hottest. But now suppose we place a wooden slab alongside the iron plate and set *anybody* to determine by touch which is the warmer of the two. If they are at a temperature near that of the air the iron will invariably feel the colder, and if near that of boiling water invariably the warmer. In the former case the difference was entirely a personal matter, depending on whose hands were warmer to begin with or had the thicker skin, while in the latter it was a genuine case of deception by the senses ; both iron and wood were at the same temperature, but the former being a good conductor abstracted heat rapidly from the hand, and gave the impression

of being colder than the wood which retained the heat from the hand in a thin layer near its surface.

In order to get rid of the latter class of errors it is usual to bring the evidence of *another* sense to bear on the facts under investigation, by employing a special device or *instrument* of some kind ; thus in the case of the iron and wood slabs we make the sense of sight available by means of a thermometer. We may, therefore, define the function of an instrument as being to confirm or contradict the evidence of one sense by that of another, or more generally to afford direct evidence of phenomena which appeal only indirectly to the unaided sense.

So far errors in observing the facts ; the next cause of failure lies in drawing wrong conclusions, and of these the most fruitful source is the want of accurate records. Amongst the practical observers from whom prognostics are derived, the best are perhaps the least likely to record their observations accurately, and after the lapse of time occurrences are retained in the memory not because of their frequency or actual importance, but because of their relative importance to the observer or the industry in which he is interested. Such errors are evidently likely to diminish the more frequently the occurrence takes place ; hence we find a very large percentage of proverbs relating to storms quite trustworthy, because gales occur in different parts of these islands some 10 to 20 times annually, while proverbs relating to seasons are seldom so reliable, only one observation a year being obtainable. In the latter case people are apt to draw premature conclusions from a small number of observations, and then to become unconsciously biased, finding confirmatory evidence where there is none, until the supposition becomes a fixed article of belief. One of the best examples of errors arising in this way is to be found in the "equinoctial gales." Careful records kept for a long series of years have shown that the probability of gales occurring

is not specially increased at or about the time of the equin-
oxes, *i.e.* that the "equinoctial gales" as such do not exist.

The belief that changes of the moon occurring at particular
hours are followed by special types of weather is so strong
and so widespread that it demands special notice.   The
following table, due in its present form to the older Herschel,
may still be found in many books of tide tables, almanacs,
and the like.

If New Moon, Second Quarter, Full Moon, or Last Quarter, happen.	Weather likely to follow during the Quarter.	
	In Summer.	In Winter.
Between		
Midnight and 2 Morning	Fair	Hard frost unless S. or W.
2 Morning ,, 4 Morning	Cold, with Showers.	Snow and stormy
4 Morning ,, 6 Morning	Rain	Snow and stormy
6 Morning ,, 8 Morning	Wind and Rain....	Stormy
8 Morning ,, 10 Morning	Changeable	{ Cold, Rain, if wind W. { Snow, if E.
10 Morning ,, 12 Noon	Frequent Showers..	Cold, with high wind
Noon ,, 2 Afternoon	Very Rainy	Snow or Rain
2 Afternoon ,, 4 Afternoon	Changeable	Fair and Mild
4 Afternoon ,, 6 Afternoon	Fair	Fair
6 Afternoon ,, 10 Afternoon	{ Fair,if wind N.W. { Rainy,ifS.orS.W.	Fair, frosty if N. or N.E. Rain or snow if S. or S.W.
10 Afternoon ,, 12 Midnight	Fair	Fair and frosty

We remark that any errors in the first column of this table
are likely to produce consequences in astronomical and tidal
matters which would at once call attention to them, and the
published data of the moon's age may accordingly be accepted as correct.   The indefiniteness of the predictions in
the second and third columns leaves a large margin for suc-
cess, but as the margin is equally large for failure, we may
assume that observations of whether the weather is "Fair,"
"Very Rainy," or "Stormy," are correct, *i.e.* that the probable errors of observation are equal in both directions.
Now, since no reservations are made with reference to disturbing influences other than that of the moon, the relation
of the weather to the lunar phases must be direct ; and, since

the latter can be calculated for any time with certainty, we ought to be able to predict the weather for any indefinite time in advance, which we cannot do. Again, since no reservation is made as to the place for which the table holds good, and since the change of the moon's phase is not a local event, the sequence of weather-changes must be everywhere the same, which it is not. Hence, it appears that the conclusions upon which the table are based are *à priori* absurd, and, therefore, even a successful prediction in any particular case cannot be more than a coincidence, as may be easily shown by comparison of predicted and observed weather.

7. *Analysis of Weather.*—Following up the suggestion of § 2, we proceed to resolve the weather into five constituent elements, limiting ourselves for the present to those which appeal directly to the senses, *i.e.* which can be recognised without any instrumental aid.

(*a*) Wind.
(*b*) { Temperature.
      { Dryness and Dampness.
(*c*) Cloud.
(*d*) Rainfall.
(*e*) "Meteors."

Since we are concerned at present only with the broader changes of weather, the detailed examination of each element may be deferred until we are in possession of better methods of observation. Certain leading facts about each, however, are evident.

Wind is motion of the atmosphere, and must therefore, like all other motions, have velocity, *i.e.* direction and speed. But since the atmosphere has mass, it must, when in motion, be capable of exerting force, and as practical experience deals most frequently with effects produced by the wind, it is usual to speak of its force rather than of its speed.

The idea of *Temperature*, or warmth and coldness, must be taken along with that of dryness or dampness, because without the help of instruments it is impossible to keep from confusing the two; moist air at a comparatively high temperature *feels* colder than dry air which may really be far below freezing-point, and the moderate heat of the tropics seems often more intense than the excessive temperatures of a desert. We may in the meantime use words or phrases describing merely the joint physiological effects, such as "damp heat," "mugginess," "closeness," "dry cold," "freshness," and the like.

Clouds may be defined as portions of the atmosphere which from natural causes have become temporarily visible. We shall find afterwards that a varying proportion of the atmosphere consists of water vapour or steam, and that under certain circumstances part of the vapour becomes condensed in the form of cloud. The classification of clouds, which usually depends on their form and height above the ground, is a matter of great difficulty. A first rough division into three classes may be made: clouds lying on the ground called mist or fog according as they are wet or dry, heavy rolled clouds at moderate elevations, and light fleecy clouds, at great heights.

Rain is taken as a generic name for moisture precipitated from the clouds by further condensation, and includes snow, hail, sleet, and "drizzle."

Under the term "meteors" we include special phenomena connected with the weather which do not directly come under any of the foregoing heads, such as dew, hoar-frost, pale or watery sun, rings or halos round the sun and moon, rainbows, thunder and lightning, aurora, etc.

8. *Example of Successive Changes.*—Selecting now a change of weather at a particular place, we may observe the

variations in the different elements, and see how far they agree with previous experience as set forth in weather lore, or how far we could have successfully predicted each stage of the change from those preceding it.

At Holyhead, on the morning of 29th June, 1890, after a few days of bright sunshiny weather with light north-westerly winds, a solar halo was observed, and the sun became pale and watery; towards afternoon the wind backed to S.W., and at six o'clock it blew a fresh breeze from S.S.W., heavy clouds banking up from the westward. The evening was damp and muggy, rain fell during the night, and the morning of the 30th broke gloomy and misty, with the wind from S., and moderately rough sea. In the course of the day the sky cleared and the wind veered again to S.W., decreasing in force until night, when it again freshened, and on the morning of July 1st was blowing in strong squalls from N. and N.W. with hard detached clouds, threatening showers at intervals, but bright, dry, invigorating atmosphere.

We note first the changes of the direction of the wind; from N.W. it gradually backed "against the sun" to S., and after blowing steadily from that point for a time, veered again to N.W. and N., becoming squally and unsteady. This reminds us of the proverb—

> "When the wind veers against the sun,
> Trust it not, for back it will run."

But, almost before the wind began to back, the sun was encircled with a halo, and became pale and watery. Since these appearances apply equally to the moon, it being merely a question of which luminary happens to be visible, we note indifferently,

> "If the sun goes pale to bed
> 'Twill rain to-morrow, it is said."

"The moon with a circle brings water in her beak."

"The sun is in his house, it will rain soon."

After the halo the sky became "dirty," and the dampness increased. In many localities such conditions cause clouds or "caps" to form round the tops of hills, hence such local proverbs as—

"When the clouds are on the hill
They'll come down by the mill."

"When Halldown has a hat,
Let Kenton beware of a skat."

"When Ruberslaw puts on his cowl,
The Dunion on his hood,
Then a' the wives of Teviotside
Ken there will be a flood."

Next, heavy soft clouds, banking up till the sky becomes overcast, are recorded, easily recognised by their lowering appearance, due to the dampness of the air, which also causes them to reflect the glare of large fires or the lights of cities : thus in Cumbrae and Bute rain is expected if the glare of the Ayrshire ironworks is seen.

The combined physiological effects of dampness and high temperature, described as "mugginess" or "closeness," is felt by all living organisms, for, as the reverend and ingenious Mr. Pointer remarks, "The very body of all animals and vegetables is (as it were) a contexture of hygrometers, barometers, and thermometers." Thus it is a sign of rainy weather when peacocks cry much, when fowls pick up their feathers with their bills, when birds that usually perch upon trees fly to their nests, when swallows fly low and skim the surface of water, or when sea-birds come in to the land.

> " If the cock goes crowing to bed
> He'll certainly rise with a watery head."

Concerning the goose—" She is no witch, or astrologer, to divine by the starres, but yet hath a shrewd guesse of rainie weather, being as good as an almanack to some that believe in her."

Again, " A bee was never caught in a shower." Wasps, gnats, and midges, are said to be more than usually vicious before rain. Rain may be expected " when sheep leap mightily and frisk about, and push at one another with their heads."

> " It is time to stack your hay and corn
> When the old donkey blows his horn."

Fishes rise more than usual, and dolphins and porpoises are specially active before rain. Many plants close their flowers and leaves on the approach of rain, as chickweed, trefoil, pimpernel, convolvulus, etc.

A muggy, close atmosphere affects the spirits and tempers of the human species, and aches, old wounds, rheumatism, and corns become painful. The damp also makes an impression on inanimate objects. Stones sweat or turn black, and wood swells so that doors and windows creak or become difficult to shut ; candle flames flare or snap ; ditches or drains smell offensively ; soot loosens and falls down the chimney ; cordage becomes taut.

Recurring now to our observations of 29th June, 1890, we find all these prognostics justified. The muggy, damp evening was followed by a night of rain, which began with mist and drizzle. This state of things continued till 8 a.m. on June 30th ; but in the forenoon came a change. The steady rain ceased with a " clearing shower," and shortly after the damp muggy feeling passed away ; patches of blue sky became visible, and the wind began to veer to westward and became squally; at 2 p.m. "Wind S.W. and sky cloudless, air dry and cool," is recorded. At 6 p.m. the wind was westerly, and during the night it veered to north, and blew in strong squalls, which continued during the whole of July 1st. These conditions are well described in the sayings :—

"When as much blue sky is seen as will make a Dutchman a jacket, the weather may be expected to clear up."

"When, after a shower, hard clouds open up overhead, leaving broken, ragged edges pointing upwards, wind will follow."

"If it begin to rain from the south, with a high wind for two or three hours, and the wind falls but the rain continues, it is like to rain twelve hours or more ; and does usually rain till a strong north wind clears the air."

"A warm wind has a cold tail." And finally,

"Do business with a man when the wind is in the north-west."

9. *Weather in Different Places : Synoptic Charts.*—Now the fact that we have been able to describe every stage in the weather-changes of the two days we have examined by means of different proverbs and sayings, many of which are to be found in the writings of Virgil, Pliny, or Aratus, and most of which are current at the present day in numberless languages and dialects, shows that the sequence observed at Holyhead at that time has been a common and frequent experience over large parts of the globe for indefinite time past. It seems, therefore, that at least one class of weather-changes follows certain broad general outlines which are independent of local conditions, and the inquiry naturally suggests itself—How are these successive changes arranged with regard to place ? Hitherto we have taken a fixed point and discussed the variations as time progressed, the next step

is obviously to take a specified instant of time and observe how the weather differs from one place to another.

The most convenient method of doing this is to mark the positions of a number of stations on a sketch map, and to fill in at each station notes of the weather observed at the time to which the map refers. This introduces us to what has proved the most efficient instrument of modern weather research, the *synoptic chart*, which enables us to see at a glance the general conditions of weather at any given instant over a large tract of country. In order to simplify and condense as far as possible the notes placed on the chart, it is convenient to have a notation or uniform system of abbreviations, the one usually adopted being that given below.

10. *Notation of Charts.*—*Wind* is represented by an arrow flying with it, thus ↑ means S., → W., ↓ N., ← E., and so on. The force of the wind is indicated by the number of barbs or feathers on the arrow, thus :—

↿ light breeze ; ↟ fresh breeze ; ↟ strong wind ; ↟ gale ; ⊙ signifies calm.

Temperature and *moisture* being usually given as numerical results of instrumental observations are omitted for the present. The remaining elements (§ 7) are described by letters and symbols as follows :—

b = ...	blue sky.
c = ...	detached opening clouds.
d = ...	drizzling rain.
f or ≋ = . .	fog.
g = ...	dark, gloomy weather.
h or ▲ = . .	hail.
l or ⦉ = . .	lightning (without thunder).
m = ...	mist.
o = ...	overcast sky.
p = ...	passing showers.
q = ...	squally.

r or ● = . . rain.

sn or * = . . snow.

T = ... thunder.

u = ... ugly, threatening.

v = ... visibility, *i.e.* distant objects appearing unusually clear.

w or ◯ = . . dew.

The above notation, devised by Admiral Beaufort, has long been in universal use in this country. The following symbols have been added more recently, and are officially recognised by the various European meteorological institutions.

⊼ . . . Thunderstorm.	∕ . . . Strong Wind.
△ . . . Soft Hail.	⊕ . . . Solar Corona.
⌴ . . . Hoar Frost.	◯ . . . Solar Halo.
V . . . Silver Thaw.	⑰ . . . Lunar Corona.
~ . . . Glazed Frost.	⑾ . . . Lunar Halo.
✛ . . . Snow Drift.	⌒ . . . Rainbow.
—→. . . Ice Crystals.	⩏ . . . Aurora.
	ω . . . Dust Haze.

Amount or intensity may be indicated by the exponents o and 2, *e.g.* :—

≈≈^{0} thin fog ; ≈≈^{2} dense fog.

11. *Application to Previous Example.*—On the morning of June 29th, 1890, we find from observations at twenty-five stations scattered over the British Isles, southerly winds in the west and north of Ireland and Scotland, westerly in the south of Ireland, and north-westerly over England, nowhere stronger than a light breeze. The weather everywhere was bright with passing clouds (*b c* in the notation), except in the west and north of Ireland, where it was overcast or showery (*o p m*). As we take this merely as a starting

point, a chart is unnecessary. Now note the observations at 6 p.m. on the same day. The general direction of the arrows at the different stations is from south-west in the southern counties, south in the midlands, and a little easterly in the north : this is more easily seen if we draw large heavy arrows following the general trend at the stations amongst which it passes, as in Fig. 1. Looking next at the weather, we find three sets of symbols, all the stations reporting "*b c*," or "*o*," or "*r*," and a study of these show that it is possible to divide the country into three quite definite belts, one where the sky is more or less covered by detached clouds, one where it is overcast, and a third where rain is actually falling (see the broken lines, Fig. 1.), which are divided by lines running nearly north and south, the cloudy area lying to the east and the rainy to the west, with overcast sky between.

Fig. 2 shows the state of things at 8 o'clock next morning. The large arrows are now as it were doubled up, showing that in the southern districts the wind has shifted more to the westward, and in the northern more to the east, while between the two little change has taken place. The distribution of weather symbols is now very different : the " cloudy " area is only represented by one station, Yarmouth, having apparently passed eastwards into the North Sea, and its former position is chiefly occupied by the " overcast " area, which now covers the whole of Scotland and the northeast of England. The rainy area has also travelled during the night from the extreme west of Ireland, and has assumed a triangular shape, covering the north-east of Ireland, Wales, and the southern, south-eastern, eastern, midland, and northwestern counties of England. In the south-west of England and Ireland the rain has been replaced by squally, cloudy weather with passing showers (*c q p*).

At 6 p.m. on June 30th (Fig. 3), the heavy arrows have become still mcre bent, forming a nearly closed curve.

Fig. 1.

Fig. 2.

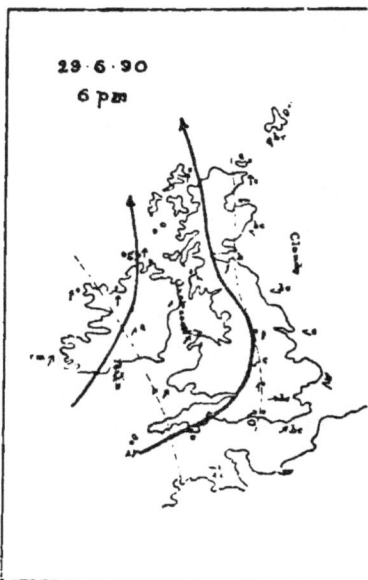

Fig. 3.

Fig. 4.

The wind in the southern districts is therefore west, in the northern east, while between them lies an eastern district over England, in which it is still southerly, and a western over Ireland, where it has changed rapidly round to north. The "overcast" area has now also disappeared, and only the apex of the rain area is left, covering the north of England and south of Scotland ; elsewhere the weather has become showery and squally. Fig. 4 shows that at eight next morning (July 1st) winds were easterly and north-easterly in the north, westerly and north-westerly in the south, and northerly between, while the rain area was limited to the north-east of England and south-east of Scotland. A narrow overcast belt intervened between it and the squally, showery area which now extended over all the southern and western parts of the kingdom.

12. *Winds Arranged in a Rotating System.*—Recurring now to the heavy wind arrows of Figs. 2, 3, and 4, if we draw perpendiculars at various points of these curves we shall find that they all intersect within a small central area around which the winds everywhere circulate in a kind of vortex, the direction in which it turns being against the sun or the hands of a watch. Hence it appears that the motion is analogous to that of a wheel revolving on its axis—there being no rotation *at* the axis, and the rate of motion, or the force of the wind, depending on the speed at which it moves round the centre.

13. *Motion of Centre.*—Having found the central area of the system for Figs. 2, 3, and 4 separately, compare its position at different times. At 8 a.m. on June 30th it lay west and north from Erris Head, on the coast of County Mayo ; at 6 p.m. off the mouth of the Mersey, and at 8 a.m. on July 1st over Lincolnshire. Joining these points we get a line showing the path of the central area, and therefore of the whole system for 24 hours, approximately a distance of 400 miles in an east-south-easterly

direction, an average of nearly 17 miles an hour, which, be it observed, has nothing to do with the force of the wind.

14. *Direction of Wind in Different parts of the System.*— Now, given the rotating system and the path of its centre, it is evident that the *direction* of the wind at any station can be found by considering simply its position with regard to that centre. Let A B (Fig. 5) represent the path of the system, O the centre at a given instant. Draw C D through O at right angles to A B. Then we have obviously three cases, according as the point of observation, P, lies *on* the path A B, or to the right, or to the left of it. Suppose a northerly or westerly wind blowing at P, as the line through the centre C D approaches, the wind will always back to some point of south; *on* the line A B it will remain steadily S.S.W.

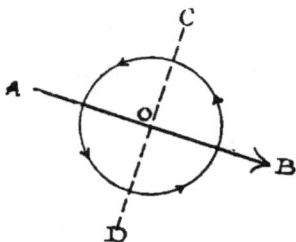

Fig. 5.

until the centre actually arrives, then after a short period of calms and variable winds it will suddenly shift to N.N.E., exactly the opposite direction, and again remain steady; to the left of A B it will blow from a south-easterly direction, shifting to east, and after the line C D has passed, to N.E.; and to the right of A B, it will shift from S.W. to W. and then to N.W.

The student must satisfy himself that this explanation really satisfies the observations charted on Figs. 2, 3, and 4; and should then study the changes of wind which would occur in the three cases if the direction of A B were N.E., E., S.E., etc.

15. *Weather in Different Parts of the System.*—Having ascertained the general system of wind circulation and its movements as a whole, let us now look how the belts of weather are placed with reference to it. In Fig. 1 the central area of the system is evidently still far to the west, although

the general change of wind shows that the British Isles are well within the outer circle. Hence it appears that the "cloudy," "overcast," and "rainy" belts are arranged in order in advance of the central area, a fact confirmed by Figs. 2 and 3, which show that these belts advance along with the wind system, and keep invariably in front of a position corresponding to the line C D in Fig. 5. We note further that the belt of squalls and showers lies *behind* the line C D for the most part, only advancing in front of it at the extreme outskirts of the system, and never approaching the line of advance.

Now observe specially that these belts are not placed symmetrically with respect to the path of the wind system. We know that the path at 8 a.m. on June 30th was E.S.E., and at that time the rain area lies chiefly in the "right front" quadrant (D O B, Fig. 5), while the overcast area is mostly in the "left front" quadrant. At 6 p.m. again, the rain area has moved considerably towards the "left front" quadrant, and the overcast area has disappeared; while at the same time the squally area has advanced relatively on the right. At eight next morning the change has progressed still further, the overcast area has reappeared, and it now lies along with the rain area, in the "left front" quadrant, the squally area having meantime spread into the "right front." But this involves one of two things, either all stations in the right front, after being warned by halos, clouds, and the like, will experience squalls and passing showers, and all those in the left rear after receiving the promised rain will return into damp, muggy weather; *or*, the whole system must have changed front by altering the direction of its path. The observations of July 2nd show that the latter event actually occurred, and at 8 a.m. the central area lay over the Cattegat, thus restoring the original arrangement of all the weather belts with regard to the different quadrants of the wind circulation.

We have therefore been able, with the help of synoptic charts, to develop from a particular case a system capable of accounting for the observed facts ; and since these facts have been shown to agree with common experience, we may for the present accept it as a typical weather system, and summarise its principal characteristics as follows :—

(1) A central calm area, around which the wind circulates in a direction opposite to that in which the hands of a watch move, the whole system progressing in a definite direction.

(2) A belt of more or less cloudy weather, in which halos, coronæ, etc., are observed (considerably in advance of the central area).

(3) A belt still in advance of the centre, but nearer to it than (2), in which the sky is overcast, and the atmosphere close, warm, and muggy.

(4) An area, generally triangular or oval, of steady continuous rain, the whole of which lies in advance of the centre, and the greater part to the right of its path.

(5) An area of bright, dry atmosphere, with squally winds and occasional showers, lying entirely in rear of the central area.

In the case discussed we have seen that the path of the system while approaching these islands was nearly E.S.E. Compare the saying—

" A rainbow at night is the shepherd's delight ;
A rainbow in the morning is the shepherd's warning."

Now a rainbow can only be observed when the sun is shining, and when rain is falling in the quarter of the sky opposite to the sun ; hence a rainbow in the morning requires that there should be clear weather to the east and foul to the west, and one in the evening clear to the west and foul to east ; from which we may argue that in the former the rain is approaching, and, in the latter, passing away, *i.e.* that an easterly course is more usual than a westerly for the system we have described ; a supposition further confirmed by—

> " Sun set in a clear,
> Easterly wind near ;
> Sun set in a bank,
> Westerly will not lack."

Hence we add—

(6) The path of the system as a whole is usually towards some point of east, at least in approaching these islands.

From (1) we may deduce at once the following practical rules :—

(1) Stand with your back to the wind, and the central area lies away to your left.

(2) If the wind blows steadily for a long time without shifting a point, expect a sudden calm and then squalls from exactly the opposite direction.

(3) If the wind shifts steadily but slowly, you are on the outskirts of the system ; if quickly, you are near the path of the centre.

These rules should be observed with a due regard to the other peculiarities of the system.

16. *Intensity of System not accounted for.*—Having stated a few empirical results and suggested a few practical applications, the question naturally arises, why should this arbitrary and apparently rather uncertain relation amongst the elements into which we have analysed the weather exist ? And again, how is it that we have been able to develop a definite system, by employing a considerable proportion of the known weather sayings and prognostics, out of a particular case which ended in nothing more serious than a moderate night's rain and a fresh sailing breeze ? How are we to distinguish such a system from one bringing

a flood or a violent hurricane? Yet again, we have seen that in changing its course, the system we have considered brought about a failure of many of what seemed the most reliable signs, no rain or wind ensuing in some quarters, while others received a double allowance. How are we to provide against such failures?

This somewhat formidable list of questions suggests that there is yet another element underlying those already apparent; one which does not appeal directly to the unaided sense, and must therefore be sought for with the aid of instruments.

But where is the other element to be looked for? On reviewing the whole evidence, it appears that the most stable and definite part of our weather system is that of the wind circulation. Hence we inquire, why does this rotational motion arise, and how is it set up? Which reminds us that we do not yet know why the wind blows at all.

CHAPTER II.

17. *Motion of the Atmosphere.*—We have defined wind as motion of the atmosphere, and may restate the question, "Why does the wind blow?" in the form, "What are the forces which set the atmosphere in motion, and how are they applied?" We shall in this chapter remind the reader of a few physical facts and principles required for our special purposes, referring him to treatises on mechanics and heat for evidence and formal proofs.

18. *Physical Constitution of the Atmosphere.*—The atmosphere consists of two quite distinct parts, or rather the earth is enveloped in two separate atmospheres—one of air and one of steam or aqueous vapour.

19. *Air.*—Air is a true gas, and consists of a mechanical mixture of about 21 parts of oxygen and 79 of nitrogen in 100 by volume, with a small quantity of carbonic acid. Since its composition is practically constant throughout the atmosphere, it need not be further inquired into. Now the distinguishing property of all gases is their power of indefinite expansion. If we introduce a small quantity of air into an empty vessel, however large, it will expand until the vessel is completely filled, and having filled, it will press upon the containing walls, trying, as it were, to expand still further.

The amount of this expansive force or *pressure* has been found for a given quantity of air to depend on the volume and the temperature, and the relations of these three quan-

23

tities to each other are expressed in two laws, known by the names of Boyle and Charles.

Boyle's Law.—The volume of a given mass of gas, kept at a constant temperature, is inversely as the pressure.

Charles' Law.—The volume of a given mass of gas, kept at a constant pressure, increases by a definite fraction of its amount for a given rise of temperature.

The density of a gas varies directly as the pressure and inversely as the volume. Regnault found the density of air at temperature 0° C. and pressure 760 mm., to be 1·293 grammes per litre.

20. *The Barometer.*—Since pressure is a *force*, it is most conveniently measured in terms of a weight. The *barometer* is simply a " weighing machine " adapted to this purpose. A glass tube, closed at one end, is filled with mercury and inverted in a vessel also containing mercury. If the instrument is now placed in the gas whose pressure is to be measured, mercury flows out of the tube until a certain point B (Fig. 6) is reached. As the part of the tube B C was originally full of mercury, and nothing has obtained access from without, the space must now be a vacuum, and no pressure can be exerted upon the mercury surface at B. Hence the column A B must just counterbalance the external pressure on the mercury in the vessel A.

Fig. 6. Now if we define a fluid as a body which offers no resistance to change of shape (thereby including both liquids and gases), the following are necessary conditions of its remaining at rest :—

(1) *The pressure exerted by any portion of the fluid is perpendicular to the surface of that portion.* It follows that we may define the *pressure at any point* of a fluid as the average pressure per unit of area on a plane surface containing the

point, and perpendicular to the pressure, when the area is supposed infinitely small.

(2) *In a fluid not acted upon by external forces, the pressure is the same at all points and in all directions.*

(3) *When the fluid is acted upon by an external force such as gravity—*

(*a*) *The pressures in the same horizontal plane are equal.*

(*b*) *The pressures at any two points differ by the weight of a cylinder of the fluid of unit sectional area, whose length is equal to the perpendicular distance between them.*

Applying these laws to the mercury at rest in the barometer, we learn that the pressure at the horizontal surface A is the same inside and outside the tube, and that the difference of pressure at the levels A and B in the tube is equal to the weight of a cylinder of mercury of unit sectional area, whose length is the vertical distance A B. But since there is no pressure in the upper part of the tube B C, this difference is the pressure we desire to measure. We shall in general express pressures in terms of the height of a column of mercury balanced by them, but in some inquiries it is often convenient to use the average pressure of the atmosphere at the earth's surface as a unit. This unit, called an atmosphere, is represented by a mercurial column 760 mm. in height at temperature 0° C. Now the mass of 1 cub. cent. of mercury is 13·596 grammes, and therefore that of a column of unit sectional area 76. cm. long is 1033.3 grammes; hence the pressure of one atmosphere is a force of 1033·3 grammes weight per square cm. = 14·7 lbs per sq. in., nearly.

21. *Specific Heat of Air.*--The specific heat of a substance is the number of units of heat required to raise the temperature of unit mass of it 1° C. In warming a quantity of air we may either keep the volume constant and allow the pressure to increase, or allow the volume to increase so that the pressure remains constant. In the latter case, it is

evident that more heat will be required, because the air has not only to be warmed 1°, but has to be expanded a given fraction of its volume. Hence we have two specific heats for air; that at constant pressure (Cp) is 0·2375, and at constant volume (Cv) 0·1684, whence $\frac{Cp}{Cv} = 1·41$.

This consideration involves the idea of a relation between heat and mechanical work. Joule found that in order to raise the temperature of unit mass of water 1° C. it was necessary to expend 424 g units of work on it, and conversely, in order to get a unit of work out of it $\frac{1}{424 g}$ units of heat must be abstracted. Suppose we expend w units of work upon a quantity of air kept at constant pressure, this is equivalent to communicating ($\frac{w}{424}$ units of heat to it, which would raise its temperature ($\frac{w}{424} \times \frac{1}{0·2375}$) = 0·010 w degrees. On the other hand, if the 1 eat in a quantity of air does w units of work in expanding, it will be cooled 0·010 w degrees.

A particular case of the dynamical heating and cooling of the air just explained, which has special interest in theoretical meteorology, is that of an ascending or descending current of air, supposed to move with such rapidity that no heat is exchanged with the atmosphere immediately surrounding.

Let a kilogramme of air ascend through a vertical distance of h metres, then the work done against gravity is $g\,h$ units equivalent to $\frac{1}{424 g} g\,h$ units of heat, which must be obtained from the air itself. If t and t_1 are the initial and final temperatures, by what precedes

$$\frac{g\,h}{424 g} = Cp \times (t - t_1)$$

or, $t - t_1 = 0·00993\ h.$

In the case of a descending current the work is, of course, done *by* gravity. Hence we may say that, *provided* no heat is lost or gained on the way, dry air is cooled or warmed 1° C. for every 100 metres of ascent or descent.

22. *Aqueous Vapour.*—If water be introduced drop by

drop into a perfectly exhausted receiver, it will be found that
the drops are evaporated as they fall, until a certain pressure
of vapour is reached, after which they retain the liquid condition.   The space inside the receiver is then said to contain *saturated* vapour, and experiment has shown that the
pressure of saturation depends only on the temperature.   If
the experiment be performed at the same temperature in a
receiver containing dry air at any pressure, exactly the same
amount of water will be taken up, only the process will
take longer, because the vapour has to make its way through
the air by diffusion.

The maximum or saturation pressures of vapour at
various temperatures were fully determined by Regnault,
and were not found to follow a simple law.   Empirical
formulæ may be devised which fairly represent the connection between temperature and the pressure of saturated
vapour, but it is better, on the whole, to employ a table.

23. *Non-saturated Vapour.*—When the amount of vapour
present in a given volume of air is not sufficient to reach the
pressure of saturation corresponding to its temperature, the
air is then partially *dry*.   Non saturated vapour behaves in
much the same way as a true gas, and closely follows to
the laws of Boyle and Charles.

24. *Saturated Vapour: The Dew Point.*—The temperature at which any given quantity of vapour becomes saturated
is called the *dew-point*, and if the temperature fall below
this point, part of the vapour is condensed into the liquid
form, until the pressure is reduced to the saturation-pressure
corresponding to the new temperature.   In like manner, if
the temperature is again raised, water is evaporated and the
state of saturation continued as long as the supply lasts,
after which the vapour becomes dry, there being no longer
enough to reach saturation pressure.   Hence a method of
determining the amount of vapour present at any time is to
cool a body having a bright surface in it until condensation

begins, which is shown by the formation of dew on the bright surface. The temperature at the surface is then that corresponding to saturation for the pressure of vapour at the time.

25. *Latent Heat.*—In order to effect the change from the liquid to the vaporous form, a certain quantity of heat is required, as is obvious if we allow damp clothes to dry on the body—the heat required for the work of drying being abstracted so rapidly from the body that most people suffer a severe chill—and on the other hand condensation liberates an equivalent amount of heat. The heat required to change the *state* of a substance is distinguished from that which goes to change its temperature by being called *latent heat*, and the quantity we are discussing is called *the latent heat of evaporation*.

26. *Supersaturated Vapour; Condensation Nuclei.*—We have thus far dealt with stable conditions, but Aitken has shown that in perfectly pure air an unstable state may be realised, in which a pressure of vapour greater than that corresponding to the temperature of saturation is maintained. In fact, condensation will not in general begin unless some nucleus is present to which the particles of water can attach themselves.

In the atmosphere the required nuclei are supplied by the impalpable dust which we know to be present even at great elevations, and it is not probable that *supersaturated* vapour, or vapour in the unstable state, occurs to any extent in nature, unless, as suggested by Von Bezold, in the case of thunderstorms or the phenomena known as cloud-bursts, where sudden falls of very heavy rain are experienced. These may be due to sudden condensation of supersaturated vapour in a dust-free region of the atmosphere, and the rise of pressure accompanying such precipitation would seem to give at least plausibility to the supposition ; but in the majority of cases the tendency is probably the other way, for it may happen that the temperature of a number of dust-particles becomes lower than that of the air in which it is floating, and vapour is condensed upon them although the air itself is not quite saturated. Much also depends on the amount of dust present, and on the size and constitution of the particles.

27. *Dry Fog.*—As water condenses on the particles of dust, their size is soon so far increased that they become visible. When the quantity of vapour condensed is small and the number of dust-particles large, or their size considerable, it is obvious that the allowance of vapour particles for each particle of dust must be small, and we have the phenomenon known as dry fog. The dry fogs peculiar to large towns are due not so much to deficient vapour as to the excessive size and quantity of the particles, which, as we know, are often sufficiently visible as smoke without the help of condensation. On the other hand, sea-fogs probably occur when there is considerable dryness, because the dust consists largely of salt particles derived from spray or surf, which greedily absorb moisture.

28. *Mist.*—When the quantity of condensed vapour becomes larger or the allowance of dust smaller, each dust particle receives more vapour, and a cloud of wet mist is formed, in which the particles are coarser and heavier than in the fog. After a certain point the dust particles are unable to retain all the moisture condensed upon them, and an unsteady condition sets in, giving rise to inequalities in the distribution of the moisture, which ends in the formation of rain-drops. The details of this process are not, however, fully understood.

29. *Radiation.*—It is now abundantly evident that the changes occurring in the various meteorological elements are ultimately dependent on changes of temperature. If the atmosphere were freed from temperature disturbances it would shortly become and would remain entirely stagnant.

Now we know that the amount of heat derived from the interior of the earth, although measurable in quantity, is insignificant in comparison with the radiant energy received from the sun, and it therefore becomes important to know what is the behaviour of the atmosphere with regard to radiation.

30. *The Sun's Rays.*—The sun sends forth rays of widely diversified wave lengths; and of each particular wave length in different quantities. It is convenient for most purposes to classify the rays according to their effects on bodies upon which they impinge; thus a certain range of wave lengths affects the retina of the eye, and gives rise to sensations of light and colour—the shorter waves to blue and violet, and the longer to orange and red, with intermediate greens and yellows; another series is remarkable for producing chemical changes in certain substances—these include the " photographic " rays, and are in general of short wave length, blue and violet, with others (ultra-violet) too short to be visible; and a third series is sensible to us as radiant heat—these chiefly of longer wave lengths, yellow and red, with " dark-heat " rays (ultra-red) too long to affect the retina. Of all rays reaching the earth's surface, those have the maximum intensity which give the eye the impression of yellow; yellow rays are both the brightest and the hottest.

31. *Effect of the Atmosphere: Absorption.*—If there were no atmosphere the amount of heat and light received at any part of the earth's surface would depend solely on the altitude of the sun, and the length of time it remained above the horizon, and the same would hold good for all the celestial bodies. The sun, moon, and planets would appear as luminous discs and the stars as points of light without any twinkling, while the rest of the sky would be perfectly dark. All places exposed to the sun's direct rays would be illuminated with dazzling brilliancy, and the heat would be intolerable, while in the shade there would be almost total

darkness, and great cold. On the other hand, while the sun was below the horizon, the earth would freely part with its heat by radiation into space, and the temperature would fall far below the freezing-point every night.

The atmosphere then acts as a kind of covering to the earth, just as clothes do to the body, tempering the fierceness of the sun's rays by day, and preventing excessive loss of heat by night. When the mingled waves of heat, light, and chemical action from the sun reach the atmosphere, a certain proportion of each is absorbed, reflected, and scattered in all directions—and the remainder transmitted directly. The relation between the amounts absorbed and transmitted depends upon what we call transparency in the case of light rays, or diathermancy in the case of heat rays. According to S. P. Langley[1] at least 40 per cent. of the radiant energy received from the sun is absorbed by the atmosphere; and this fraction diffused in all directions illuminates the sky, makes objects in shadow visible, and extending into regions beyond the sun's direct rays, gives rise to the phenomena of twilight.

But the proportions absorbed and transmitted are very different for different wave lengths; the atmosphere is much more transparent to red rays than to blue and violet. On a very clear day, when a comparatively large proportion of all rays are transmitted, the atmosphere is scarcely able to arrest any but blue rays, and the sky therefore has a very intense blue colour; while in hazy weather not only blue but green and yellow rays are stopped, the sky has a sickly yellowish colour, and at the same time the sun appears red, the only light rays able to penetrate being of that colour. It is easy to see that when the sun is in the zenith the rays from it traverse the shortest possible (*i.e.* the vertical) path through the atmosphere, and that, as it sinks towards the horizon that path becomes longer and longer, so that there

---

[1] *Phil. Mag.* 1884. II. p. 289.

must be more and more absorption. Hence the sun's disc most frequently appears red just after sunrise or just before sunset.

Little is as yet known with certainty about the nature of this process of absorption. It is believed that pure dry air is almost quite transparent to all the sun's rays, and it seems likely that dry unsaturated vapour has little absorptive power. The investigations of Crova go far to show that the absorbing element is in the first place the dust. Aitken found that dust particles exposed to the action of heat rays experienced very slight changes of temperature—provided they were small enough—so that a cloud of dust was not warmed by sunshine unless the particles of which it was composed were comparatively large. Again, Crova has been able to photograph invisible clouds—clouds which emitted rays too short in wave-length to be sensible to the eye, but which nevertheless produced chemical effects. These facts suggest that the excessively minute particles of dust are able to reflect and scatter the chemical and violet rays, but that it is only when their size is increased by the condensation of moisture upon them that they are able to arrest the yellow and red and the heat rays. When the particles become large enough to be visible as dry fog, we have seen that only red and heat rays are transmitted—and when they are sufficiently large to form cloud, radiation is almost entirely stopped. It must be remarked, however, that the proportion of rays transmitted does not increase regularly with the wave-length, certain selected rays of special wave-lengths being almost entirely stopped; these give rise to dark "telluric" bands at different parts of the solar spectrum.

Crova has found that in summer the intensity of solar radiation increases steadily for some hours after sunrise, then suddenly becomes very irregular, changing rapidly from minute to minute, decreasing on the whole till some time after mid-day, when it again increases, and, after reaching its maximum, diminishes till sunset. He suggests that the un-steadiness begins when the sun's warmth becomes sufficient to cause a considerable increase in the evaporation of water from the soil, which condenses on the dust particles in the air, increasing their size and causing a haze which checks the intensity at mid-day. As the heating process continues, the water is evaporated from the dust particles, again reduc-ing their size and allowing freer transmission. In winter, when the quantity of vapour is small, the curve of solar in-tensity shows only a single maximum at noon.

We thus see that if the air is dry and clear, compara-tively little of the sun's heat is stopped on its way through the atmosphere, and most of the changes of temperature are brought about by heat communicated from the earth's surface in a manner we shall presently discuss. But a dampness insufficient to form visible haze may nevertheless increase the size of the dust particles sufficiently to cause considerable absorption and radiation of heat in the atmo-sphere, and consequent variations of temperature. We may thus account for the fact that the variation of temperature in the air over the ocean is some four times as great as in the surface water of the ocean itself.[1]

Hence also we find that temperature changes as we ascend in the atmosphere at a rate depending chiefly on the heat received from that surface. The usual condition is such that temperature falls as the elevation increases at an average rate of $1°$ C. per 163 metres. This gradient is, however, liable to very great variation ; it may be steeper or less steep, or it may be reversed, as when a layer of cold air lies next the ground. In any case the distribution of temperature becomes more uniform at great heights. Observe that we are not here dealing with ascending or descending currents.

32. *Transmission of Rays.*—The transmitted rays may be

[1] *Challenger* Reports. " Atmospheric Circulation," p. 7.

considered separately according as they fall upon the sea or upon land.

In the former case the rays are partly reflected, partly absorbed near the surface, and partly transmitted through the water. The observations made during the cruise of H.M.S. *Challenger* show that some rays penetrate to a depth of 500 feet below the surface. On account of this transmission, and also because of the high specific heat of water, the changes of temperature over the ocean are small, and take place slowly. The "daily range" of air temperature —the difference between the hottest part of the day and the coldest part of the night—and the "annual range" are small, the nights and winters are warm, and the days and summers cool compared with those on land.

The heat received on a land surface is also in part reflected, but the remainder is wholly arrested by the thin exposed layer, which is quite opaque, and on account of its low specific heat becomes much heated : the rise of temperature depends of course largely on the nature of the surface— if the substance composing the surface stratum is a good conductor, the heat is quickly transferred to a lower stratum and the warming of the surface checked ; if it is a bad conductor, the heat is retained at the surface, which may then attain a very high temperature. Dense heavy clay soils are much better conductors than loose sandy ones, because the latter imprison large quantities of air, which is a bad conductor ; hence extremes of heat and cold penetrate to a much greater depth in clay than in sand. Vegetation also acts as a protective covering to the soil, and its temperature never becomes very high, partly because the heat is used up in evaporating moisture from the plants, and partly because they present a large surface to the air, which when heated moves away and is replaced by colder air.[1] The changes of temperature are therefore more rapid and of greater range

[1] Buchan : *Handy Book of Meteorology*, p, 83.

over the land than over the sea—least over clay soils or regions covered with vegetation, and excessive over arid sandy deserts and bare rocks.

33. *Terrestrial Radiation.*—Since, on the whole, the temperature at the earth's surface from year to year is the same, it is evident that an amount of heat exactly equivalent to that received must be lost by radiation into space ; and since the heat radiated back into space has to pass through the atmosphere in the same way as that received, it is evidently subject to the same conditions with regard to transparency, When the atmosphere is clear and dry, nocturnal radiation goes on freely, and the surface of the earth is rapidly cooled just as by day it is rapidly heated ; and the same conditions of haze or cloud which cut off the sun's rays by day prevent loss of heat by night. Again, surfaces which absorb heat freely radiate freely, and hence the nights are relatively warmer over the sea than over the land, and over clay soils than over sandy.

34. *Air Temperature : Dew.*—We must now look a little more closely into the manner in which the changes of temperature at the earth's surface are communicated to the atmosphere. Air, especially if it be dry, is a very bad conductor of heat, and therefore if the atmosphere remained motionless the thin layer immediately in contact with the earth would quickly take the temperature of its surface. This is very much what happens on a calm, clear night when the soil is cooled by radiation; the stratum of air lying next the surface is cooled by contact, sometimes to very low temperatures, and as it becomes colder it becomes heavier and has no tendency to move away if the surface be level. When the temperature falls below a certain point the vapour rising from warm under-layers through the pores of the soil or amongst the blades of grass is condensed on this thin surface layer, either as water, when it forms dew, or as ice when it is called hoar-frost. Hence we see why dew and hoar-

frost are associated not with cloudy, damp weather, but with clear skies and little wind, when there is free radiation. Even after prolonged dry weather it is found that the ground exudes moisture to form dew on the tips of grass blades and the under sides of stones ; but we must be careful to distinguish between the pearly deposit which is the genuine dew, and the "sparkling dew-drop" hanging on the leaves, which is not dew at all, but water expired by the leaves themselves.[1]

During the day, when the earth's surface is warmed by the sun's rays, the action is somewhat different. Part of the heat is propagated from the surface downwards by conduction as a wave, at a rate depending, as we have seen, on the conductivity of the soil, the daily variation of temperature being sensible to a depth of about four feet. The heat not drained off by conduction warms the thin stratum of air lying just in contact with the surface—but this air being now warmer than the layer above it, is lighter, and, rising, is replaced by more cold air, which in its turn is warmed, rises, and is replaced. Hence, "convection currents" are set up, and the atmosphere is warmed to a considerable elevation.

In what precedes, we have for the sake of clearness supposed the air to be perfectly clear and dry—or rather have neglected the heat absorbed in transmission. Since a body radiates heat just in proportion as it absorbs it, it is evident that a damp, dusty layer of air behaves much in the same way as a water surface, so that we have the two effects as it were superposed ; the temperature of the damp air is changed by the heat absorbed or radiated by it, and also by that from the earth's surface, which has already been transmitted through it.

35. *Diurnal Variation : Temperature.*—This prepares us for a *daily variation* of the physical conditions of the atmosphere—in the first place, of the temperature, and through

Aitken : *Trans., R.S.E.*, vol. xxxiii., p. 29.

the temperature of the pressure, humidity, and other elements indirectly, depending on the intensity of the sun's rays, and on the length of the day. It is usual to discuss these variations with reference to their daily mean—the theoretical value of which is the average of all the values for every instant during the day—although for practical purposes the average of twenty-four hourly values is sufficiently accurate.

The daily curve of temperature, although varying considerably in different parts of the world, is in general of a simple form. Over the open sea, in the North Atlantic, the *Challenger*[1] observations showed that the minimum occurs about 5 a.m. and the maximum about 2 p.m., and this may be taken as fairly representative. Near the equator, where the days and nights are nearly equal throughout the year, there is little difference in the daily curve at different seasons; thus Batavia gives minimum 5.50 a.m., maximum 1.20 p.m. In higher latitudes, where the days vary greatly in length, the hours at which these phases occur differ considerably. During summer the maximum usually occurs between 2 and 4 p.m., unless, as in some places, sea-winds tend to increase cloudiness towards the afternoon, when the maximum occurs earlier; and during winter the maximum is almost always about an hour earlier than in summer. The minimum during summer occurs just at dawn, and, therefore, earlier in high latitudes than in low. The first rays of the sun striking the upper strata of the atmosphere are reflected to the ground and absorbed by it, so that the air becomes slightly warmed before sunrise. When the ground is covered with snow, there is very little absorption of the reflected rays, and temperature does not begin to rise till the sun is above the horizon.

Sir David Brewster showed that in general if the tempera-

[1] *Challenger* Reports, " Atmospheric Circulation," p. 7.

ture is above the average for the day at any given hour, it
will be nearly as much below it twelve hours later. We
may therefore obtain a close approximation to the true mean
temperature for the day by taking the average of observations at two hours of the same name, as 3 a.m. and 3 p.m.,
or 10 a.m. and 10 p.m. The best results are obtained at
hours when the temperature is not much different from the
actual average ; 9 a.m. and 9 p.m. are those usually adopted
in this country.

Another method of determining the mean temperature is
from observations of self-registering thermometers, which record the highest and lowest extremes for the day ; the mean
of these is usually about half a degree higher than the
average of twenty-four hourly observations. The reading of
the maximum thermometer *minus* that of the minimum
gives us another extremely important element of climate, the
daily range of temperature. This depends chiefly upon
proximity to the sea ; in mid-Atlantic it amounts to about
1°·8 C., increasing to 2°·4 near land; while in dry, continental
climates it may average 15° or more.

36. *Diurnal Changes of Pressure.*—The diurnal oscilla-
tions of atmospheric pressure show in general two maxima
and two minima, the former at 10 a.m. and 10 p.m., and
the latter at 4 a.m. and 4 p.m. These four phases are most
sharply defined and of greatest amplitude in low latitudes
and in damp climates. At stations near the sea, especially on
the west coasts of continents and islands, it is found further,
that in summer the morning maximum and the afternoon
minimum are delayed, and the former becomes unusually
large, while the latter is greatly diminished. At continental
stations, again, the morning maximum occurs early in the
day, and is much diminished, while the afternoon minimum,
although still delayed, is increased in amplitude.

The occurrence of this double wave over the ocean, the
surface temperature of which remains nearly constant

during the day, proves that it is not caused by variations of temperature of the earth's surface, but of the atmosphere itself; it depends on the varying amounts of heat absorbed and transmitted according to the size and quantity of the atmospheric dust particles.

37. *Seasonal Variations.*—The seasonal variations of the meteorological elements are in many respects analogous to the diurnal phenomena we have just described. The earth gains heat in the daytime of summer, loses it during the night of winter, and passes through the transition stages in the morning of spring, and the evening of autumn. Just as the daily changes of temperature are least near the equator and greatest in higher latitudes, least over the sea and greatest over continents, so in the tropics the seasons are scarcely marked; in the temperate and frigid zones they oscillate through a wide range; over the sea winters are mild and summers cool, and over the continents intense cold alternates with burning heat. From the nature of the case we do not find the double diurnal oscillation of pressure reproduced in the seasons : the conditions are for the most part determined by the temperature. In summer the land is warmer than the sea, and pressure is accordingly lower over the former; while in winter the sea is warmer than the land, and the distribution of pressure reversed.

38. *Corrections for Daily and Monthly Range.*—We are not at present concerned to pursue this subject further. Our object so far has been to ascertain the normal condition of things, to separate out the processes which are always going on from hour to hour and day to day, for diurnal and seasonal variations are always taking place under all circumstances and conditions. We thus come to regard not only the infinite small variations which are constantly taking place from minute to minute throughout the atmosphere, but all storms, moving systems such as that described in Chapter I, and spells of fine weather and

the like, as *disturbances*, occurring over and above the
normal march of events.   Hence in discussing, for example,
a disturbance of temperature or pressure, we cannot compare observations made at different hours of the day, or on
different dates, until they have been corrected for daily or
monthly range as the case may be, which is usually accomplished by reducing all to the mean for the day or
month.   It may, of course, happen that the disturbance is
so great that the diurnal variation is a negligible quantity in
comparison with it ; in temperate regions the diurnal variation of pressure is small and comparatively unimportant for
many purposes, but in the tropics it is of greater amplitude
than most disturbances, and cannot be overlooked.

39. *Position of Bodies on the Earth's Surface : Absolute
Motion.*—Any body on the surface of the earth is subjected
to the action of two principal forces, that of gravitation or
the earth's attraction and the so-called centrifugal force due to
the earth's rotation on its axis.

Now, Newton showed that in the case of a sphere, the
attraction of gravity acts as if the whole mass were collected
at the centre, and this result holds good, to a close approximation, for the earth ; and again, we know that a
body revolving in a circle tends to increase its distance
from the centre.   But the circles described by bodies at
rest on the earth's surface are circles of latitude, and therefore the centrifugal force will act in the direction of a line
drawn from the earth's axis of rotation perpendicular to it,
that is, it will act vertically upwards at the equator, horizontally near the poles, and in some intermediate direction at
all intermediate latitudes.   Hence, for all intermediate
latitudes we may resolve the centrifugal force into two parts
—one vertically upwards, and another horizontal—the latter
always tending towards the equator.   The vertical component is obviously counteracted by gravity—but how
about the second ?   What prevents a free body such as the

water in the sea from moving towards the equator ?   Unless
we introduce some new force altogether, the answer must
clearly be that gravity does not act vertically—and that
there must be a horizontal component sufficient, and just
sufficient, to counteract the centrifugal force.   But it was
stated that gravity acted towards the centre of the earth,
hence a vertical line downwards from the earth's surface
cannot pass through the centre unless it be drawn from the
equator or the poles, which is the same as saying that the
earth is not a sphere, but a spheroid.

Fig. 7 will make this clearer.   Let O be the centre of the
earth, O F a radius
of the equator, and
N the pole.   Then
at a point P in lati-
tude P O F, A P
B is the horizon-
tal plane and C
P D the vertical.
On   account   of
the earth's rotation
about   N   O,   P
moves in a circle
perpendicular   to
the plane of the
paper whose centre
is   G, and radius

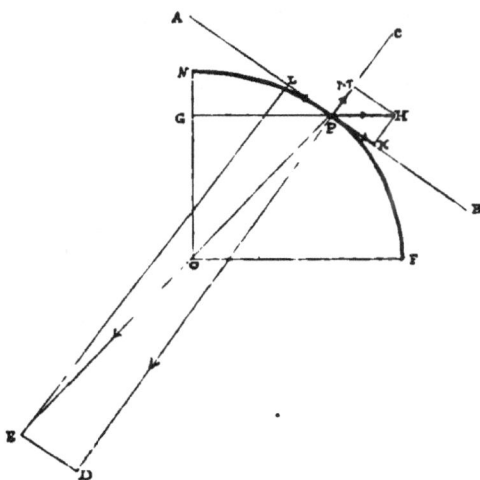

Fig. 7.

G P, and the centrifugal force acts along P H.   Resolving
P H in the horizontal and vertical planes, we get P K and
P M.   Again, let P E represent the force of gravity ; then
if P E, which must pass through O, is not in the plane of
C P D, we may resolve it in that plane and in A P B, as
P D and P L.   Then if P, being free, is to remain at rest,
P L must equal P K.   It is evident that if P E be perpen-
dicular to A P B—i.e. if N P F be the arc of a circle—there
can be no force P L.

40. *The Force of Gravity.*—It is important to note that g, the force of gravity at any place, is represented by P D – P M. Since forces are, in general, measured with reference to g, it is necessary to have a standard value, which is usually that of the 45th parallel of latitude, and is equal to 9·8061 (metres). Its value at any other point is easily found from the following empirical equation.

$$g = 9\text{·}8061 \, (1 - \text{·}00260 \, \cos 2 \, \varphi) \, (1 - \tfrac{h}{3006720}).$$

When φ is the latitude, and h the height above sea level in metres.

41. *Relative Motion on the Earth's Surface.*—Now suppose the point P to move on the earth's surface. Then since the earth rotates from west to east, if P moves in an easterly direction it is really moving faster than the earth, and if in a westerly, slower; hence in the first case the centrifugal force will be greater than is counterbalanced by the ellipticity of the earth, and P will tend to move towards the equator; while in the second the centrifugal force will be less, and the horizontal component of gravity will tend to turn P towards the pole. Thus the rotation of the earth always tends to turn a moving body, which may of course be a current of air, to the *right* in the northern hemisphere, and to the *left* in the southern. This law is now often called Ferrel's Law.

42. *Friction*—In concluding this chapter, we must remind the student that a current of air experiences considerable resistance from friction. On the earth's surface this is of course least over the ocean, and greatest over a mountainous country. For obvious reasons the coefficients of friction cannot be determined once for all in the laboratory, but only by observation in each particular case. It must not be forgotten that there are also considerable frictional effects between currents of air moving in different directions at different altitudes. The operation of these frictional effects will be more easily understood in the treatment of the particular case given in the next chapter; in the meantime

it must be borne in mind, especially by the student of the applications of mathematical formulæ to meteorology, that the difficulties in the way of absolute numerical determinations of the coefficients are enormous, a fact which has been rather lost sight of by critics of such applications in this country.

CHAPTER III.

CYCLONES.

43. *Isobars and Gradients.*—In Chapter I. we attempted to sift out certain facts concerning one particular type of disturbance, as far as was possible from a study of horizontal motions only. Let us proceed to inquire what distribution of pressure will account for the observed horizontal circulation, and then test our method by comparison with actual readings of the barometer.

It will be necessary in this case to deal with distribution of pressure over a large area, and therefore convenient to employ the method of a synoptic chart by noting simultaneous readings of the barometer at different points. We may then draw lines through series of points having the same barometric reading, which gives us a system of contours of heights of the barometer. Let Fig. 8 represent a series of such lines drawn at intervals of o·1 inch. Then it is evident that by drawing a line as A B everywhere perpendicular to the contours or *isobars* as they are called, we can find the steepness or gradient, as A′ B′ in the lower part of the figure, which represents the variations of pressure along A B. In the same way as we measure a railway gradient as 1 in 50, 1 in 200, and so on, we say barometric gra-

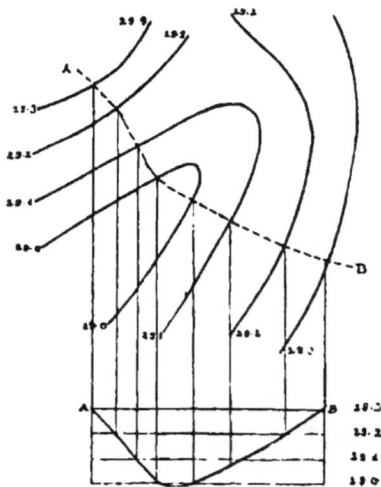

Fig. 8.

dients are so many thousandths of an inch in 15 miles,
or so many millimetres in one degree of the meridian or
111 kilometres.

44. *Gradients and Winds.*—Now, the force which causes
the atmosphere to move or produce the wind, evidently acts
" down " the gradient, from the points of higher pressure to
those of lower. Hence the problem of Chapter I. becomes,
What forms of isobars, or what direction of gradients will

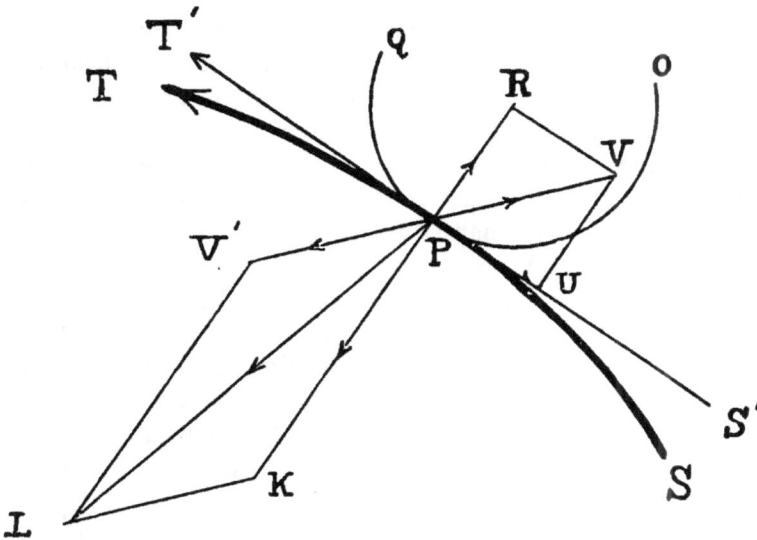

Fig. 9.

give, under the known conditions, the observed wind circulation? Let S P T (Fig 9) be any part of one of the thick wind
arrows of Figs. 1 to 4. At P the air is moving in the direction of S′ P T′. The forces resisting this motion are two :
that due to the earth's rotation which, by Ferrel's law, tends
to make it move in a circle O P Q whose centre is R, and
that due to friction, which simply tends to prevent any
motion at all. These two forces, therefore, act in directions
P R, P S′; let them be represented by P R, P U. Then, if the

velocity is uniform, the force of the gradient must be such that the resultant P V of P R and P U is counteracted, and at the same time there must be a force P K perpendicular to S' P T' proportional to the curvature of the path S P T at P, the latter being required to counteract the centrifugal force in S P T. Hence, taking P V backwards, the force required must lie in some direction P L, the resultant of P V' and P K. That is, stand with your back to the wind, and the lowest pressure lies to your left and in front. Or, since the isobars are perpendicular to the gradients, we may say the wind moves nearly along the isobars but tends to cross from the higher to the lower ones. We observe that the force tending to make the angle between gradient and wind less than 90° is due to the component required to overcome the friction on the earth's surface, and is therefore small in the case described in Chapter I. where the system has come from the ocean. We may, indeed, not be much surprised to find the wind directions nearly parallel to the isobars.

45. *Example of Low Pressure System or Cyclone.*—Figs. 10, 11, 12, and 13 show the distribution of pressure at the times corresponding to Figs. 1-4. We observe in Fig. 10 a fairly uniform barometric slope towards north-west, and as expected, the wind blowing nearly along the isobars, but turning slightly inwards towards the lowest pressures. Fig. 11 exhibits a similar arrangement ; and Fig. 12 brings us to the root of the matter by showing the nature of the who'e system. The central calm area is the region of lowest pressure ; the isobars are arranged concentrically around it, and in accordance with our prediction, the wind blows in a direction everywhere *nearly* parallel to the isobars, but tending towards the lower pressure. Finally, we observe from Fig. 13 that the system of lower pressure has moved in the same way as that of wind circulation, still further confirming the connection between the two.

We have thus arrived at what is evidently a much more

Fig. 10

Fig. 11

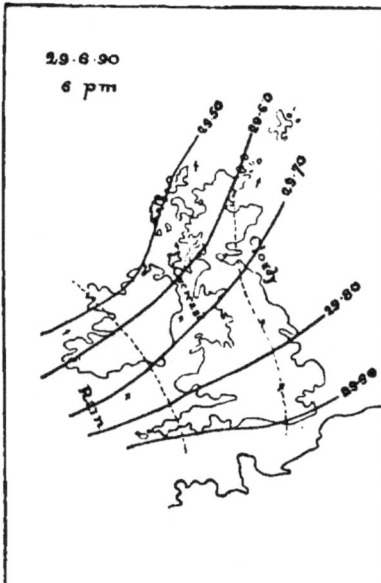

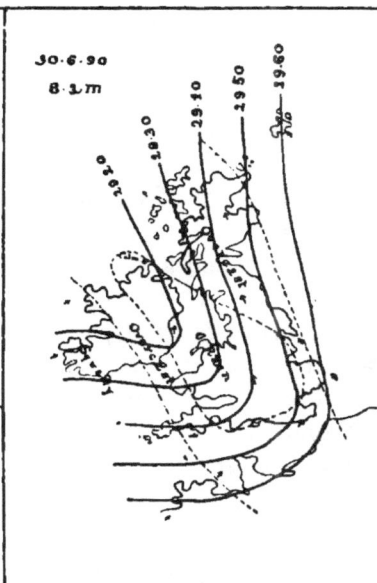

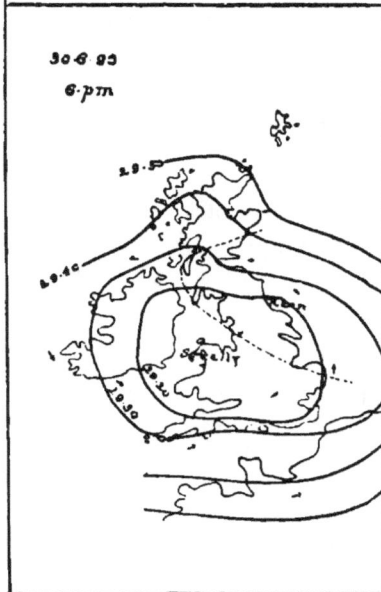

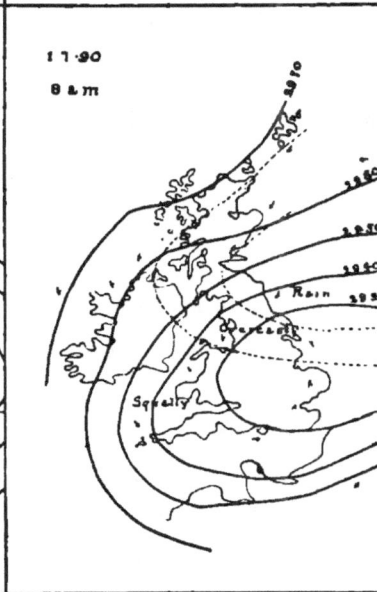

Fi 12.

Fig. 13.

satisfactory method of defining the system described in Chapter I., for instead of merely recording the directions in which the wind blows, we can ascertain the forces which cause it to blow, and we now know something about how these forces act. We may, therefore, in future begin by inquiring as to the forms of the isobars and then discuss particular types of weather associated with them.

The area of low pressure, and the whole system connected with it, is called a " cyclone " or " depression ; " in America simply a " low."

46. *Intensity of Cyclones.*—It is evident that in a depression the actual pressure or height of the barometer is a matter of little moment ; the forces involved are due to the gradients or *differences* of pressure, and are greater the steeper the gradients. Hence a cyclone is of the mild type described in Chapter I., or attains to a gale or hurricane just as the gradients are gentle or steep. An excellent example of this fact is given by the great storm which passed over Edinburgh on January 24th, 1868. The lowest reading of the barometer recorded was 29·29 inches, only 0·6 in. below the average for the month. The following table gives approximately the gradients for the day :—

Hour.				Gradient.			
9 a.m.,	.	.	.	1 inch in 3,333 miles.			
Noon,	.	.	.	1	,,	124	,,
2 p.m.,	.	.	.	1	,,	78	,,
3 p.m.,	.	.	.	1	,,	84	,,
4 p.m.,	.	.	.	1	,,	107	,,
8 p.m.,	.	.	.	1	,,	196	,,
9 p.m.,	.	.·	.	1	,,	513	,,

A terrific hurricane raged from eleven till six o'clock, and between noon and 4 p.m. much damage was done to trees and buildings, corresponding exactly with the times of steepest gradient.[1]

If we study the barometer changes at different points in the path of a cyclone, it is at once obvious that in the "front" of the depression the barometer is everywhere falling, while in the "rear" it is everywhere rising ; and we thus have the turning point along the line C D (Fig. 5), which

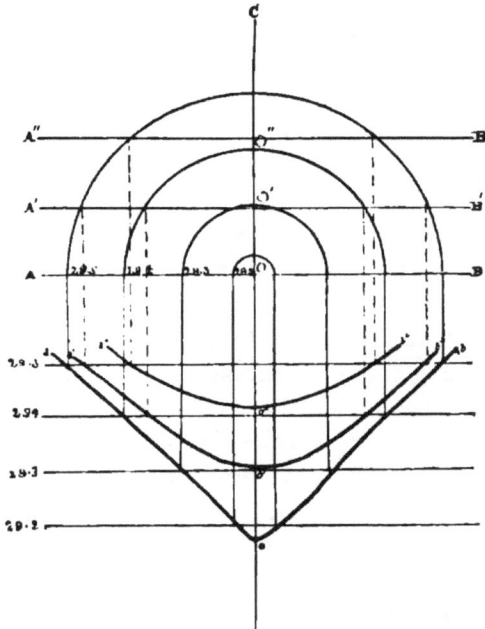

Fig. 14.

is called the "trough" of the cyclone. This leads to one of the main difficulties in the use of the barometer at an isolated station. If the observing station lies on the line A B, the barometer will fall until the centre O passes, and the line B O evidently lies directly along the gradient. But if the station lies to one side of A B, the direction is not along, but partly across, the gradient, and it is therefore

[1] T. Stevenson in *Good Words*, 1868, p. 366.

impossible to form an accurate estimate of the steepness. Let A and B (Fig. 14) correspond to the same letters in Fig. 5. Then if we draw isobars at intervals of o·1 inch we may take stations lying on paths A B, A′ B′, and A″ B.″ A B being perpendicular to the isobars, lies along the gradient, but A′ B′ and A″ B″ lie more or less across it. The lines *a o b, a′ o′ b′, a″ o″ b″* show the record that would be made by a self-registering barometer; observe that in each case the barometer turns on the line *o C*, the trough of the cyclone, but the fall is less as we recede from A B. If we imagine the figure to represent a plan of a cup-shaped hollow in the ground the isobars are simply contour lines, and the barometer curves *a b, a′ b′*, and *a″ b″* sections along A B, A′ B′, and A″ B″.

Yet another difficulty must be taken into account. We cannot judge of the steepness of the gradient merely by the rate at which the barometer falls at any particular station; for this evidently depends on the rate at which the depression is passing. In Fig. 14, the barometer at O stands about o·3 inch lower than at B, but the rate at which it falls is determined by the speed with which O travels towards B, just as two men starting at the same time from the top of a hill may reach the foot at the same moment, although one has climbed slowly down a precipitous face, and the other run full speed down a gentle slope.

47. *Path of the Wind in Cyclones.*—In discussing the forces which come into play when air is set in motion by a difference of pressure, we found that the angle between the wind direction and the gradient was slightly less than a right angle, and that the deficiency from 90° was due to the friction of the earth's surface, so that the greater the friction the smaller the angle. We found, further, that in a system travelling over the ocean the friction was so slight that the wind direction seemed to follow a path in many places nearly parallel to the isobars. So much is this the

case in most cyclones passing over the British Islands that rules drawn up for practical purposes usually ignore the defect from a right angle altogether, and assume that the wind blows perpendicular to the gradient, *i.e.* along the isobars. Thus Buys Ballot's Law is usually stated, "Stand with your back to the wind and the lowest barometer lies to the left"; nothing is said about the front.

But while we do not in this way introduce serious error in

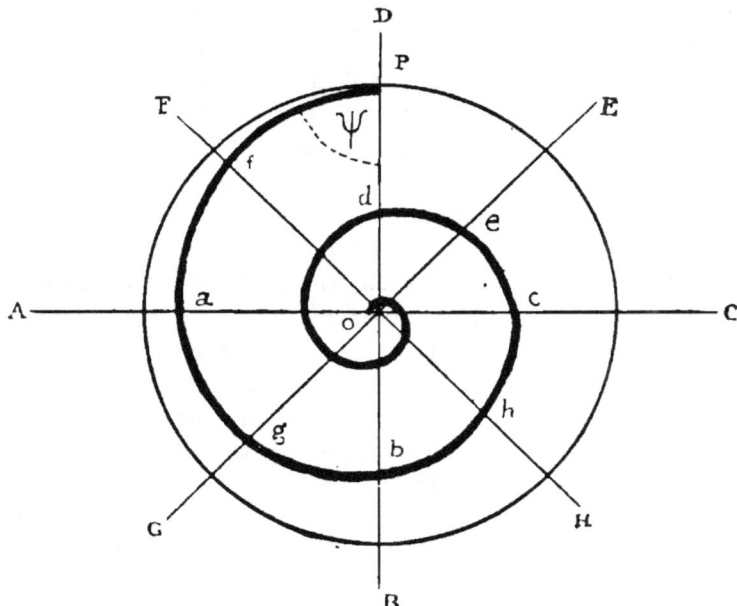

Fig. 15.

practical calculations about the British Islands, the omission of the last clause would in many parts of the world be simply disastrous; and in all cases it is inaccurate.

Consider in detail the path of the wind when the isobars are concentric circles, and the gradients therefore slope radially towards a central point, and when the direction of the wind makes a constant angle ψ, less than 90°, with the gradient. Let A B C D (Fig. 15) represent one of the isobars (O the centre) ; then at any point P the air is moving in a direction P f, making an angle ψ with O P ; it thus arrives, say, at f. But at f it still travels at an angle ψ with $o\ f$, and so on. Hence the path is the curve called a logarithmic spiral.

We are accordingly led to conclude that in a cyclone the air moves towards the centre in a spiral, and we observe again that the angle ψ at which the incurving takes place depends, other things being equal, on the friction between the air currents, and the earth's surface, being smaller, the greater the friction. The value of ψ must also be different at different parts of the globe, since the deflecting force, due to the earth's rotation, is not everywhere the same. If the earth were at rest the wind would simply blow radially in all directions towards the centre.

48. *Influence of Circulation on the Gradient.*—We have hitherto considered the gradient as a given force, which may serve to explain the facts observed. But the wind circulation in a cyclone must clearly react to a greater or less extent upon the gradient. We may compare the motion of any particle of air in a cyclone to that of a stone whirled at the end of a string, the string being meanwhile drawn in by being wound round a stick. We know that as the string gets shorter the stone revolves faster ; and Newton proved that in such a case stone and string describe equal areas in equal times. But the "centrifugal force" counteracted by the tension on the string increases as the square root of the cube of the increase of velocity. Hence, applying this to the air in a cyclone, it appears that the air tends more and more to keep away from the centre, and we must therefore have a decrease of pressure, the gradient becoming steeper and steeper near the centre.

49. *Vertical Circulation in the Atmosphere: Condition of Equilibrium.*—Granting that the air in a cyclone does move in towards the centre, what becomes of it when the cen-

tral area is reached? Involved along with this is the further question—What causes the central force which gives rise to the cyclone? Evidently the only path open to the air from the central area is in an upward direction.

The condition of rest, as stated in § 20, is that the pressures at any two points differ by the weight of a cylinder of unit sectional area, whose length is equal to the perpendicular distance between them. Since a column of air 1 sq. cm. in section and 1 cm. in height at temperature 0° C. and barometric pressure 760 mm. weighs ·001293 grammes, we can easily calculate the height of the atmosphere supposing the density to be the same at all levels; the average weight is 1033·3 grammes, hence the height $\frac{1033\cdot3}{0\cdot1293}$ cm. = 7993 metres. This is called the "height of the homogeneous atmosphere."

But the density varies as the pressure; and since the pressure in any horizontal layer is simply the weight of the layers above it as there is no rigid enclosing shell, the air must become less and less dense as we ascend. Let fig. 16 represent a column of air of 1 square metre section, whose total weight at the earth's surface is P; and let it be supposed that the temperature is the same throughout. Then if p_1 is the pressure at a height of h metres, and p_2 that at $(h-1)$ metres, p_2-p_1 evidently represents the weight of 1 cubic metre at the pressure p_1 to a close approximation. Call this weight W_1; then since the density is proportional to the pressure we may put $W_1 = Cp_1$. Similarly, we have for a height of $h-1$ metres $W_2 = Cp_2$, for $h-2$ metres $W_3 = Cp_3$, and so on. Hence we get

Fig 16.

$$p_1\, C = p_2 - p_1$$

$$p_2\, C = p_3 - p_2$$

and so on.

$$\frac{p_2}{p_1} = C + 1$$

$$\frac{p_3}{p_2} = C + 1$$

and so on.

Multiplying the left sides and right sides of the latter series together, we get, remembering that $P = f_1 + f_2 + f_3 + \cdots$,

$$\frac{P}{f_1} = (1 + C)^h$$

From the known properties[1] of damp air we can easily determine the values of W_1 for different conditions of temperature and moisture, whence we can find an expression for C. In this way, the above formula becomes, after all reductions have been made,

$$h = 18401 \cdot 2 \left(1 + \cdot 00367 \frac{t + t'}{2}\right) \left(1 + \cdot 378 \frac{e}{p}\right)$$

$$\times \left(1 \times \cdot 0026 \cos 2 \varphi\right) \left(1 - \frac{Z}{5096720}\right) \log \frac{P}{p}$$

where h = difference of levels between the two stations in metres.

t = temperature   }
P = pressure   } at lower station.

t' = temperature }
p = pressure   } at upper station.

e = pressure of vapour.

φ = the latitude.

Z = the mean of heights of the two stations above sea-level.

This gives, then, the relation between pressures at different elevations; and by assuming the conditions at a particular time to be those of equilibrium, the formula may be used to measure heights.

50. *Ascending Currents, Stable, Unstable, and Indifferent States.*—Suppose now that from any cause an ascending current is initiated at the earth's surface; then we have seen (§ 21) that if the air is perfectly dry, it will be cooled nearly 1° C. for every 100 metres of ascent. Hence there are three possible cases with reference to the normal gradient or rate of cooling of the surrounding air (p. 33).

[1] See Sprung, *Lehrbuch der Meteorologie*, p. 67.

1° The fall of temperature may be less than 1° C. per 100 metres.

2° It may be exactly 1° C.

3° It may be greater than 1° C.

In the first case, supposing the ascending current to start from the earth's surface at the same temperature as the surrounding air, when it reaches the height of 100 metres it will be colder than the air surrounding it and therefore heavier; consequently the ascending motion will be diminished.

In the second case, since the temperature in the ascending current falls at the same rate, the relative conditions simply remain the same at all elevations.

In the third, the surrounding air having cooled faster than the ascending current, the latter will be warmer than it at the height of 100 metres, and the tendency to ascend will be increased.

When the air is, as of course always happens, more or less moist, the ascending current cools a little more slowly. If the ascending motion continues until the temperature of saturation is reached the rate of cooling suffers a further sudden diminution, for the air is warmed by the latent heat set free, and the ascending force correspondingly increased. An initial higher temperature evidently still further favours the continued ascent.

It appears, then, that if from any cause an ascending current is established, there are certain definite conditions depending partly on the temperature gradient and partly on the original strength of the ascending current, which determine whether the ascending motion is to continue and increase or not. If it continues, it is evident that the requirements of a cyclone are satisfied, for the removal of air by the ascending current causes a diminution of pressure, and the surrounding air tends to flow in from all sides, and we see that a severe storm may easily be developed by the action of forces due to the earth's rotation on a quite inconsiderable disturbance. When the normal gradient is such that the ascending motion is checked, the atmosphere is said to be in the *stable* state; where the ascending motion is encouraged, *unstable*; and where the gradient is the same as that in the ascending current, the condition is said to be *indifferent*.

A striking illustration of the facts just explained may be taken from the records of the Ben Nevis High and Low Level Observatories, which is of special interest as it indicates a line full of rich promise of a quite new method of weather forecasting, which may one day supersede that of synoptic charts. According to these observations the mean rate of fall of temperature with increase of elevation is 0°·63 C. per 100 metres. Now the mean temperature of the low level observatory is 8° C.; hence a current of air starting at a temperature of 10° C. will on an average be denser than the surrounding air when it reaches a height of about 850 metres, if we suppose that it cools 0°·9 C. for every 100 metres of ascent. But the observations at the two stations show that an unusually rapid decrease of temperature with height, especially when conjoined with an unusually slow decrease of pressure with height, are " frequent concomitants and precursors of storms."[1] This means that the conditions are favourable to the maintenance of ascending currents.

51. *Condensation: Special Centres of Energy.*— We have seen that if condensation begins while the ascending air is still at a fairly high temperature, the tendency to ascend is markedly increased. But as condensation goes on, and less vapour is left in the air, the rate at which the temperature falls increases again. And it is matter of observation that at considerable heights above the earth's surface, the normal temperature gradient becomes very much less. Hence the

---

[1] *Trans. R.S.E.* xxxiv., p. xlix.

"indifferent" state must ultimately be reached, and that probably at no very great height. It is worth noting that there is in general a special centre of energy in the part of the ascending column between the point where condensation commences and that where the indifferent stage is reached. This part of the column will be at a greater elevation the drier the air supplied to the column originally. A peculiarity of the storms of Indian seas may probably be explained in this way : it is found that in the rainy season when the air is everywhere nearly saturated, storms which approach the land are easily broken up and destroyed on meeting even a comparatively low range of hills ; while the storms preceding and following the rains may cross a considerable tract of country and emerge upon the ocean undiminished in strength.

52. *Descending Currents: Anti-Cyclones.*—Whatever quantity of air ascends to the upper regions of the atmosphere, an equal quantity must ultimately descend to take its place. The continued up-draught of air must cause an excess of pressure in the higher strata, and hence a tendency to settle down. We thus have a system established which is exactly the opposite of a cyclone ; an area of high pressure, fed by the air flowing out from the ascending current, in which the air tends to descend. In our preliminary inquiries about the cyclone we had the problem—given the circulation to find the forces : the present question is—given the force, find the circulation. If the earth were at rest, the air would on reaching the earth's surface flow directly from the area of high pressure to that of lower ; but by Ferrel's Law it is in the northern hemisphere deflected to the right : hence the circulation is the opposite to that in a cyclone, the direction of motion being *with* the hands of a watch, and at the same time tending away from the centre of high pressure. Systems of this description are called anti-cyclones.

53. *Origin of Cyclones.*—It appears, then, that the essential part of the cyclone is a central ascending current, and we have seen that under certain conditions the environment of the current may be such as to materially strengthen it, and under certain others to weaken it. Our information with regard to the upper strata of the atmosphere is unfortunately very incomplete ; it is derived chiefly from observations of the movements of clouds and the records of high level observatories. The two most important series of cloud observations are those of Ley and Hildebrandsson, which agree in showing that the direction of the lower clouds is somewhat to the *right* of the surface winds, nearly parallel to the isobars, while the highest or cirrus clouds show a marked tendency to move away from the centre, their direction of motion being still further to the right. Observations at high level stations on the Alps have shown that in the central area of a cyclone the temperature gradient closely agrees with what we have been led to expect in an ascending current.[1] Again, Hann has found unmistakable evidence of descending currents in anti-cyclones.[2]

So much concerning cyclones we may therefore take as established by observation ; but we are obviously left with the formidable question—What causes the ascending current necessary for the cyclone ?—and it may be said that this question is as yet unanswered. Until recently what is known as the convection theory was believed to give a fairly satisfactory solution, and in the hands of mathematical meteorologists, and especially of the late Professor Ferrel, it served to explain many important phenomena. The substance of it was briefly this : given an *unstable* vertical temperature gradient, if at any place on the earth's surface the air becomes slightly warmer than in the immediate neighbourhood, it will ascend, and on account of the sur-

---

[1] *Met. Zeit.*, 1890, p. 332.
[2] *Ibid.*, 1890, p. 227.

rounding gradient the ascending motion will continue and increase, until a cyclone is developed. The ascent will continue until the gradients become indifferent, when on account of the higher pressure the gyrations will be reversed and become anti-cyclonic. From this anti-cyclone, colder, denser air will radiate and slowly settle down on all sides of the ascending current. This theory involves the condition that the temperature gradient, in the area surrounding the cyclone, shall be unstable—that the ascending current shall be warmer than the normal, and the descending current in the anti-cyclone colder. There can be no doubt that when these conditions exist they are specially favourable, and it must be admitted that with unstable conditions a cyclone will develop more energy than *ceteris paribus* it would be likely to do otherwise. But Hann[1] and others have shown conclusively that cyclones frequently occur when the gradient is far from being unstable, and not only so, but that the ascending current in cyclones is often not warmer, but colder than the descending current in anti-cyclones; facts in themselves fatal to the convection theory in so far as it attempts to account for the origin of *all* cyclones. We have, in addition, the fact that cyclones do not occur with the greatest frequency in summer, when on account of the warming of the earth's surface the gradients are oftenest unstable and excessive heating over local areas is most likely to take place.

It seems probable that the true cause of ascending and descending currents is to be looked for in the great movements of the atmosphere as a whole ; and in particular at the interfaces between different main streams in the general circulation. It is known that in different parts of the world cyclones tend, at different seasons of the year, to follow certain paths, and these paths appear to be directly or indirectly connected with movements on a larger scale.

[1] *Sitzb. der K. Akad. der Wiss.* 1890.

Helmholtz[1] has recently shown that a comparatively rare upper current blowing along a dense under current, in the same way as the wind blows over the surface of the sea, will cause waves measuring many miles from trough to trough—and if the under current be supposed sufficiently shallow, we can imagine that the air at the bottom, *i.e.* on the earth's surface, may be seriously disturbed. The mathematical difficulties involved in such problems are, however, so great that a complete solution is still far out of reach.

Having now discussed in some detail the mechanism of an ideal cyclone, supposed exactly circular, and stationary in position, we shall be the better able to understand the bearings of further facts concerning the systems which commonly occur. We have begun by satisfying ourselves of the truth of certain facts, employing a method of probabilities —then by the help of known physical laws we have been able to predict certain other phenomena, developing in this way a theory of cyclones which although admittedly incomplete has nevertheless shown itself useful in enabling us to understand the main features of these disturbances. We return to the method of probabilities, but are now in a position to make a more accurate use of it by making numerous *measurements* of the same thing and calculating the most probable value : we may for example find the relative conditions of temperature in the front and rear of cyclones by observing the readings of the thermometer in a large number of cases and taking the most probable value, which in such a case is the average.

54. *Form of Cyclones: Direction of Longest Diameter: Size.*—Cyclones are not in general circular, but oval. Loomis[2] found that on an average of three years the ratio of the longest diameter to the shortest was 1·94 in the

---

[1] *Sitzb. der Berliner Akademie.* 1889, p. 503.
[2] *Contributions to Meteorology,* 1885, pp. 7, 8.

United States and 1·70 in the Atlantic Ocean; and in more than half the cases 1·5. Van Bebber [1] found that in 77 European cyclones the average ratio was 1·78, with a tendency to be more circular in winter and more oval in summer. According to the same investigators the longest diameter of cyclones in the United States or in Europe lies in a direction nearly W.S.W. to E.N.E. in a very large majority of cases, while over the Atlantic the direction varies within considerable limits.

It is scarcely possible to fix a superior limit to the size of cyclones; the area covered may be several thousand miles across. But when the dimensions become great, particularly if the system is much elongated, the cyclone frequently breaks up into two, three, or even more separate centres of depression, each with its own particular system of wind circulation, between which are belts of calms or light variable winds. When such subdivision takes place one of the centres usually increases in depth and intensity at the expense of the others, which fill up and disappear. Hence we may have a violent storm of comparatively small area developed from a cyclone of small intensity but great extent. Such changes may occur with great rapidity, so that it is sometimes impossible to identify the same cyclone on two synoptic charts drawn at an interval of only a few hours. We have here obviously a fruitful source of failure in weather forecasting; all the symptoms of an approaching cyclone may be exhibited and the prognostics falsified by the filling up of the depression—or the weather of a cyclone front may be experienced without being followed by the conditions characteristic of the rear. It is further evident that large cyclones must be modified in form and position by the variations of the deflecting force due to the earth's rotation in different parts of it, arising from difference of latitude.

[1] *Handbuch der Ausübenden Witterungskunde*, pt. II., p. 221.

It may be said that the average size of cyclones is greater the higher the latitude. Tropical cyclones are in general smaller than those of the temperate zones, and more symmetrical in shape; their diameter does not often exceed 500 miles, and on an average the shape of the isobars is more nearly circular. Small cyclones must not, however, be confounded with waterspouts or tornadoes, which are too small to be sensibly affected by the rotation of the earth, and may revolve in either direction; these are special phenomena of a quite distinct nature.

55. *Gradients and Observed Winds.*—In our discussion of the mechanism of an ideal cyclone we saw that with any given gradient there is associated a wind velocity whose direction and speed depend on the deflecting force due to the earth's rotation, and on the frictional resistance offered by the earth's surface and by other masses of air. There are therefore, a number of unknown quantities introduced in the shape of coefficients of friction which make it difficult, if not impossible, to calculate numerical values of wind velocity from given gradients by the help of theoretical formulæ. Hence we merely state that the changes of wind velocity with given changes of gradient are found under favourable circumstances to justify the assumptions on which the formulæ are based, thereby confirming the correctness of the theory—and proceed to the numerical results of observation.

Loomis[1] gives the following results for cyclones over the North Atlantic Ocean. The mean latitude of the centres of these depressions was 58°·48', and the measurements were made at the part of the cyclone where the gradients were steepest.

[1] *Contributions to Meteorology*, p. 127.

Isobars.	Latitude N.	G.	Velocity.	Inclination.
715-720	58°·0'	4·17	15·90	25°·24'
720-725	57·36	3·87	16·21	26·30
725-730	57·12	3·71	16·14	27·54
730-735	56·48	3·60	16·08	29·54
735-740	56·24	3·52	16·14	31·54
740-745	55·54	3·45	16·27	33·18
745-750	55·30	3·37	16·27	33·42
750-755	55·0	3·24	15·84	34·6
755-760	54·30	3·10	14·73	34·48

The first column gives the two isobars between which the measurements are made, the second their mean latitude, the third the gradient expressed in millimetres per degree of the meridian (111 kilometres), the fourth the velocity in metres per second, and the fifth the angle between the tangent to the isobars and the direction of the wind, reckoned towards the centre.

The investigations of Ley[1] showed that in general a given gradient is associated with stronger wind in summer than in winter; thus for Kew he obtained the following results :—

Gradient	.	.	. 6	9	12	15	18	21	24
Velocity (m. per sec.) Winter			1·8	2·3	3·4	5·0	6·3	6·8	8·0
Do. do. Summer			2·9	3·9	5·0	6·4	7·5	8·1	9·4

Ley[2] further found that with a given gradient northerly and easterly winds are markedly stronger than westerly or southerly, results fully confirmed by Sprung[3] for stations on the German coasts. The angle between the direction of the wind and the isobars is given by Ley[4] as 13° for coast stations, and 29° for inland stations, thus showing distinctly the increased effects of friction on land. The mean of these,

[1] *Qu. Jour. Roy. Met. Soc.*, III. p. 232.
[2] *Nature*, vol. xxiv., p. 8.
[3] *Archiv der Deutschen Seewarte*, II., 1879.
[4] *Jour. Scot. Met. Soc.*, vol. iv., 1873, p. 72.

21°, agrees exactly with the value for Denmark given by Hoffmeyer[1], whose investigations also show a higher value for southerly and easterly, *i.e. land* winds, than for northerly and westerly. Loomis[2] gives for the eastern part of the United States a mean inclination in cyclones of 47°, the greatest values being for north or north-west winds, which are, in this case, the land winds.

The researches of Ley, Hildebrandsson, and others, have shown that in the cyclones of Western Europe, at least, the gradient is seldom, if ever, symmetrical round the centre, being in four out of every five cases steepest in the quadrant between S.E. and S.W. of the centre, and least in that be-

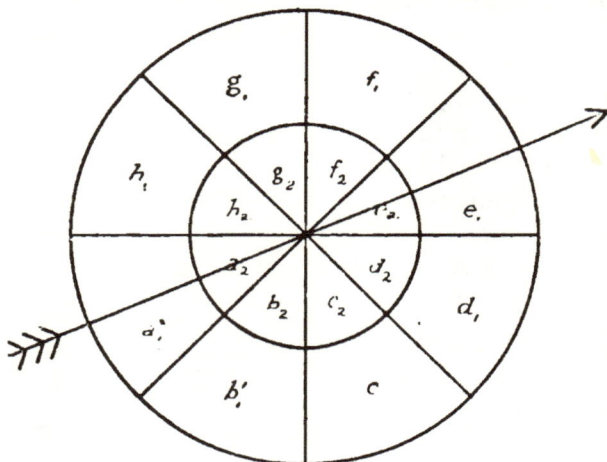

Fig. 17.

tween N.E. and N.W. Further, it is found that the in-curving of the wind from the isobars towards the centre is greatest in the front of the cyclone, and least in the rear. Ley[3] divided the cyclone area into eight outer and eight inner segments, as shown in Fig. 17, and gives the following averages for the angles of incurving. The arrow shows the cyclone's line of advance.

[1] *Met. Zeit.*, xiii., 338.   [2] *Amer. Jour. of Science*, 1874.
[3] *Q. J. Met. Soc.*, 1877.

Segment.	Angle.	Segment.	Angle.
a_1	11°	a_2	13°
b_1	14°	b_2	16°
c_1	24°	c_2	26°
d_1	36°	d_2	35°
e_1	42°	e_2	32°
f_1	38°	f_2	37°
g_1	28°	g_2	25°
h_1	10°	h_2	9°
Mean	25°·24′	Mean	24°6′

It is now generally admitted that the warm moist southerly winds in the front of the cyclones of Western Europe are the principal source from which the system derives its energy; they are the real feeders of the ascending current, and therefore it is not surprising to find a stronger indraft there than occurs in the case of the colder, drier northerly and north-easterly winds in the rear.

56. *Distribution of Pressure at Higher Levels.*—This leads to another consequence of the higher temperature of the air flowing into the front of a cyclone than of that flowing into the rear. Pressure must evidently decrease more rapidly with height in the colder, denser air than in the warmer; and, therefore, in any horizontal plane at, say, 1,000 metres elevation, the form of the isobars will not be the same as at the earth's surface, but pressure will be relatively lower on the northern and western sides, and the centre will be displaced northwards. From observations of cirrus clouds, Ley[1] found that in the British Isles the centre was not only so displaced but also lagged behind at higher levels.

57. *Inclination of Winds at Higher Levels.*—We have already stated (§ 55) that observation confirmed the supposition that in the higher part of a cyclone the air flowed away from the centre. The following table gives the average angle between the isobars at the surface and the direction

[1] *Q. J. Met. Soc.*, 1887.

E

of the upper currents, shown by the motion of cirrus clouds,
as determined by Ley.   The letters refer to the segments of
Fig 17, and the angles are this time reckoned positive *away*
from the centre.

Segment.	Angle.	Segment.	Angle.
a_1	6°	a_2	0°
b_1	11°	b_2	—39°
c_1	34°	c_2	—17°
d_1	56°	d_2	12°
e_1	62°	e_2	45°
f_1	73°	f_2	40°
g_1	—95°	g_2	82°
h_1	9°	h_2	16°
Mean	19°·30′		17°·24′

It appears from these numbers that, just as the inflow of
air at the surface is greatest on the front and right-hand
segments, so at the cirrus level the outflow is greatest in the
same segments.   Ley concludes accordingly that the south-
easterly winds probably extend to only about half the elevation of the northerly winds on the left side of the cyclone,
and further explains the excessive outflow on the right side by
the fact that the great majority of our cyclones are associated
with an anti-cyclone lying to the right of them, the down-
current of which is fed by the air ascending in the cyclone.
We may note here the fact that the cirrus clouds observed
in this outflowing current are often the first indication given
of an approaching cyclone ; it is well known that mare's-
tail clouds moving from the north-west frequently precede
storms.

58. *Distribution of Temperature and Rainfall.*—The distribution of temperature at the earth's surface in a cyclone
is in great part determined by the direction of the wind ; the
southerly winds in the front raise it above the average, and the

northerly winds in the rear depress it. Along with this the effect of the increased cloudiness in checking radiation must be taken into account; in summer the diminished sunshine keeps the temperature below the average, while in winter the loss of heat into space is in a measure prevented, and temperature remains above the normal.

The position of the rain area and of the ring of low cloud which surrounds it varies considerably, but the researches of Loomis, Abercromby and others show decidedly that

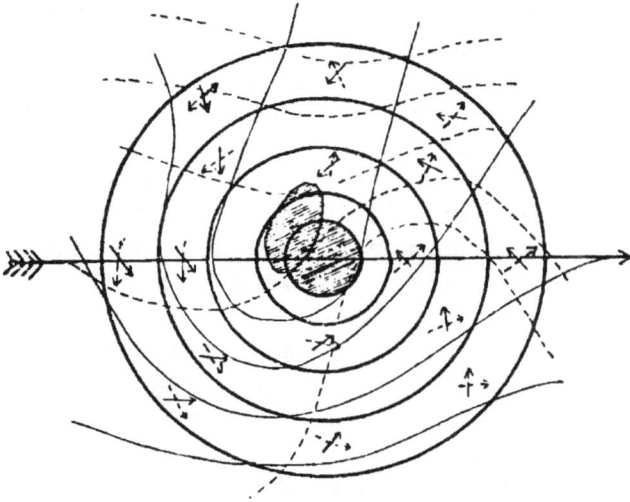

Fig. 18.

while primarily related to the centre of the cyclone it generally extends furthest to the right front. The depression described in Chapter I. affords a good example of this.

59. *Summary: Diagram of Typical Cyclone.*—The best summary of the knowledge we have so far gained concerning cyclones may be given in Fig. 18 (modified from one due to Moller[1]), which represents a system moving eastward.

[1] *Ann. der Hydr.*, 1882.

The heavy black lines indicate the isobars, the heavy arrows the wind directions, and the dotted lines the isothermals at sea level.   The light lines and arrows give the isobars and wind directions at the level of the cirrus clouds.   The shaded areas indicate the regions of lowest pressure in each case.

60. *Motion of Cyclones: Cyclone Tracks.* — Beginning with the cyclones of Western Europe, the first and most important fact established by Ley is, that by far the greater number of cyclones move in an easterly direction : when a westward motion occurs it is usually slow and seldom continues for any length of time.   The researches of Abercromby, Köppen, and Van Bebber have since shown that certain definite tracks can be laid down, along which cyclone centres tend to move, and that particular tracks are specially frequented during each season of the year.   The following is a summary of the principal results obtained by the last-named investigator from a discussion covering the period 1875-90.

Route I. begins to north-west of the Outer Hebrides and runs in a north-easterly direction along the coast of Norway, till it cuts the Arctic Circle, where it divides.   This route is much frequented at all times of the year, but especially in autumn and winter.

Route II. runs from north of the Shetland Isles to the Gulf of Finland.   Not very frequently followed.

Route III. starts somewhat further north than II., and runs either to the Skagerak or central Sweden.   After reaching the Baltic, cyclones following this track take either an easterly or south-easterly course : and they almost invariably occur between September and March.

Route IV. extends from the mouth of the English Channel to the Gulf of Finland, and is chiefly followed by shallow depressions during the summer months, although severe

—————————————
[1] *Met. Zeit.*, 1891, p. 361.

winter storms sometimes take this path, as for example the great blizzard of March 9th and 10th, 1891.

Route V. also commences at the mouth of the English Channel, and runs south-eastwards parallel to Route III. to the gulf of Genoa, where it divides into three, one branch turning northwards through Switzerland to the Baltic provinces of Russia, a second going eastwards to the Black Sea, and a third curving southwards into the Mediterranean. This track is most frequently followed during the winter months.

These five principal routes vary somewhat in position from month to month, and it must, of course, be understood that there are, unfortunately for successful weather prediction, a considerable number of depressions which do not follow any of them consistently. Van Bebber, however, may be said to have finally established the two following laws with reference to the general conditions prevailing in the area affected by a depression, which practically embody the results obtained by Ley in 1872.

1° The advance of a depression takes place in a direction perpendicular to the line of steepest gradient, so that the highest pressure lies to the right. Observe that this accords with what we know of the motion of the upper currents feeding anti-cyclonic areas to the right of the cyclone.

2° Depressions usually move so that the temperature is highest to the right of their track.

The first law plays the more important part in winter, and the second in summer.

61. *Types of Weather.*—We can thus understand that the weather of western Europe is in great part determined by the relative pressures and temperatures over three great areas ; the central part of the North Atlantic, the northern part in the neighbourhood of Iceland and the continent of Europe. It is found that the Iceland area is almost always one of relatively low pressure, hence the tendency of cyclones

to move eastwards, keeping the higher pressure on the right. Again (§ 39) pressure is relatively higher over the land than over the sea in winter, and the reverse in summer, hence on the whole depressions tend to skirt along the coast in winter, and penetrate more easily inland in summer, the path being, however, considerably modified by the distribution of temperature in the warmer season. Such considerations have led to the classification of weather into a number of types, each of which is distinguished by the prevalence of cyclones following special tracks in succession. When, as frequently happens, the general distribution of temperature and pressure remains constant, a particular type of weather may persist for a considerable period, giving rise to prolonged spells of weather ; and in these circumstances regions lying outside the cyclone tracks may have settled fine weather for weeks together while the districts traversed by them experience a continued succession of disturbances.

62. *Storms.*—The percentage of depressions in which winds of dangerous violence are developed depends very largely on the influence of land. We observe that nearly all the main cyclone tracks tend to skirt along the coast or to pass over inland seas, probably on account of the smaller frictional resistance offered to their motion. But the air drawn in by the depression from a land area must evidently contain much less vapour than that over the ocean, and we accordingly find a marked inclination to diminish in intensity. Thus from an examination of 154 cyclones Van Bebber [1] found that, while 65 per cent. occasioned gales in the British Islands, only 32 per cent. retained dangerous energy till they reached the coast of Germany. The records of the British Meteorological Office [2] show that on the west of Ireland, the north-west of Scotland, and the south-west of England, all of which lie in the neighbourhood of great

---

[1] *Handbuch, pt.* II., p. 265.
[2] *Report of the Meteorological Council*, 1887, p. 22.

storm tracks, about twenty severe gales occur annually, while in the north-east and east of England the number is about eleven. On the whole, serious disturbances are most likely to follow one of the main routes.

63. *Rate of Motion of Cyclones.*—The rate of advance of depressions varies within very wide limits. Van Bebber gives, as the average of 1676 cases, a mean velocity of 27 km. per hour, the highest average occurring in October (31 km.), the lowest in August (23 km.). He finds further that at all times of the year depressions following the main tracks usually move with considerably greater velocity than "erratics," the highest averages being for Routes I., III., and V.

It may be said that on the whole deep depressions move faster than shallow, although the difference is not by any means strongly marked. A much closer relation is observed between the *change* of depth of a depression and its velocity of translation. A cyclone which is increasing in depth and intensity moves with increasing velocity, and conversely; and we have further the remarkable fact, that one which maintains a constant depth moves in general slower than one which is gradually becoming shallower, unless the rate of filling up is extremely rapid.

64. *Relation of Winds to Rate of Advance.*—We have stated in a former paragraph that the velocity of the wind in a cyclone is not apparently appreciably affected by its motion of translation. If we consider the case of a depression travelling eastwards, we should expect an easterly component in the winds throughout the whole system which might produce important effects in a shallow depression moving with considerable velocity. The effect would evidently be to cause outflowing winds in the front of the system, and to increase the incurving in the rear; again, in the central calm area, we should find a wind corresponding in direction and speed to the velocity of the system.

But the incurving of the wind is greatest in front and least in rear, and the wind required in the central area is never observed. It therefore seems probable, as suggested by Sprung,[1] that at least in the lower layers of the atmosphere, the air is not moved forward in the cyclone in its progress, but that the system is of the nature of a wave disturbance, always affecting new masses of air.

65. *Special Cyclone Areas.*—It may be laid down as a general rule that cyclones generally move in an easterly direction in all parts of the northern hemisphere north of lat. 30°. According to Loomis the average rate of motion over the Atlantic Ocean is 29 kilometres per hour, and over the United States, 45·7 kilometres, or nearly double that observed in Europe. So far as is known, cyclonic storms seldom or never originate within 5° of the equator. The intermediate tropical belt is, however, the scene of the most violent hurricanes known, especially in the neighbourhood of the West Indies and in the Indian and China Seas. The West Indian cyclones, most of which have their origin between 10° and 20° N. lat., usually move in a westerly or north-westerly direction until they approach the thirtieth parallel, when the path curves round by north towards east, their average rate of progress westwards being 24 kilometres per hour. In the Indian Ocean and China Sea the nature and distribution of storms vary at different seasons of the year in a manner too complex to be given in detail here. The course of cyclones is, in general, westerly during its first part, and it may or may not recurve eastwards, the average rate of motion being still slower than in the West Indies.

---

[1] *Lehrbuch,* p. 246.

CHAPTER IV.

66. *Anti-Cyclones.* — In describing cyclonic systems we had occasion to point out that the ascending currents must be compensated by equivalent descending currents, and that a wind circulation was associated with the descending current, which was in every respect the antithesis of the cyclone.

It is to be observed at the outset that anti-cyclones differ very greatly from cyclones in *intensity*. The air is absorbing heat and increasing in capacity for moisture as it descends, and therefore no energy is available in the form of heat. Again, the deflecting force of the earth's rotation acts on a mass moving away from a centre instead of towards it ; hence there is no tendency for the rotational velocity to increase, as in the cyclone, on account of the principle of equal areas.[1] Anti-cyclonic systems are therefore in general ill-defined in shape, the barometric gradients are slight, and the normal wind-circulation disturbed and disguised by local or accidental causes. It is, therefore, rather unprofitable to discuss such questions as the average inclination of the winds to the isobars with the same detail as we have done in the case of cyclones. We shall merely state a few leading features.

The characteristic circulation is, as already shown, exactly the reverse of a cyclone ; in the same direction as the hands of a watch, spirally outwards from the centre at the earth's surface, and inwards towards it at the level of cirrus clouds. Like cyclones, anti-cyclones are not in general circular, but

[1] § 48.

oval. An area of high pressure, however, sometimes becomes very much elongated when placed between two
depressions. The most frequent direction of the longest
axis is in the United States nearly the same as in the case
of cyclones, N. 44° E. Over the Atlantic Ocean and Europe
the commonest direction is N. 75° E., nearly 40° more to
the eastward than that found for low pressure systems.
Just as in cyclones, a high pressure area when much
elongated has sometimes two or three distinct centres of
circulation ; but there is not the tendency for one of these
to grow in intensity at the expense of the others for which
cyclones are remarkable.

67. *Permanent and Recurrent Anti-Cyclones.*—We have
seen (§ 61) that in the North Atlantic pressure is per-
manently low over an area in the neighbourhood of Iceland,
and increases as we go southward. The maximum is
reached near latitude 32° N., and again decreases towards
the equator. There is in fact a permanent area of high
pressure over that ocean, usually called the "Atlantic Anti-
Cyclone," which varies in extent and intensity from month
to month in accordance with the principles explained in
§ 39, attaining its greatest development in summer, and
least in winter.

On the south-eastern side of this system, there are
accordingly permanent north-easterly and easterly winds,
the *north-east trades*, extending from 30° N. lat. to about
7° N. lat. On its northern side, the Atlantic anti-cyclone
merging into the low pressure area near Iceland, gives rise
to the prevailing westerly winds of the North Atlantic and
Western Europe, and frequently penetrates over the Iberian
Peninsula and Southern Europe, especially during the
summer months, sometimes extending northwards over the
British Isles.

Again, over the vast land surface of Asia and Eastern
Europe pressure is excessive during winter, and circulation

anti-cyclonic. This immense system sometimes includes the whole of north-western Europe, but in general is only connected with the Atlantic anti-cyclone by a ridge of high pressure in Southern Europe—known to meteorologists as the "Continental axis."

68. *Relation of Anti-Cyclones to Adjacent Cyclones.*— It appears that there are two large areas of high pressure, the centres of which are practically immovable, but which vary in extent and intensity according to the season of the year, one being strongest and most fully developed when the other is weakest; and these combine to give a north-westerly gradient directed towards a stationary low centre near Iceland. We have already seen how these areas govern the motions of cyclones, which tend to skirt round their borders, following one another in succession, and breaking into them with difficulty. It is important to notice that there may thus be a number of cyclones "feeding" one high pressure area at the same time; and further, that while the one system compensates the other in the matter of transferring air from one level to another, there is no mutual relation in the sense of cause and effect. Cyclones of great intensity are not in general associated with areas of extraordinarily high pressure, and an unusually high barometric maximum most frequently corresponds to a minimum of only moderate depth. Loomis,[1] to whose investigations this result is due, suggests as a reason for it the fact, that the average breadth of high-pressure areas is nearly proportional to the barometric gradient, from which it would follow that air does not flow more rapidly from a system in which pressures are excessive, than from one in which they are moderate.

69. *Moving Anti-Cyclones.*—While the weather of western Europe is almost completely controlled by the great high

---

[1] *Contributions to Meteorology*, p. 89.

pressure areas we have described, smaller systems are not infrequently developed, and these are perhaps more strictly the antitheses of the true cyclone than the larger ones, which are really integral parts of the general circulation of the atmosphere as a whole. These systems vary greatly in extent and position, and move slowly and irregularly from place to place, generally, however, in an easterly or south-easterly direction. Loomis gives their mean velocity at 13 kilometres per hour, but they not infrequently remain stationary for days together. They may indeed be treated as merely off-shoots separated from the large high pressure systems, with which they usually reunite sooner or later.[1]

In the United States the great controlling areas of high pressure are absent, and the anti-cyclones therefore stand in more direct relation to depressions. Loomis found that in a great majority of cases anti-cyclones were pre-ceded and followed by areas of low pressure—the average distance from the high centre to the low being 2371 miles on the east side, and 2381 miles on the west, and the gradient twice as steep in the former case as in the latter. The average breadth of the anti-cyclones measured was 2587 miles, and the mean direction of their path S. 40° E. with a velocity of about 34 kilometres per hour; more to the southward and less rapid than in the case of cyclones.

70. *Weather in Anti-Cyclones: "Radiation" Weather.*— The weather conditions accompanying anti-cyclones are determined by the descending current. The air which dur-ing its previous ascent was to a great extent deprived of its aqueous vapour, and probably also washed free of a large proportion of its dust, is in its descent warmed by compres-sion, and therefore at the same time dried. It accordingly becomes very transparent to radiations of all kinds, which are freely transmitted from the sun to the surface of the earth or the thin layer of air lying in contact with it, and back

[1] See Van Bebber, *Lehrbuch der Meteorologie*, p. 277.

again into space. Hence we have in the anti-cyclonic area
clear, cloudless skies, and at the earth's surface wide ranges
of temperature. In winter, when high pressure areas attain
their fullest development over land, the temperature of the
lowest strata of the atmosphere is extremely low. Loomis
found that in 74 cases over Eurasia the average temperature
was—28°·3 C., at 7 a.m. Washington time, corresponding
to the warmest part of the day; or 10°·6 C. below the mean
temperature. The persistence of these anti-cyclones over
Siberia gives rise to some of the lowest temperatures observed.
At Verkhoyansk the average during the month of January is
—48°·8 C. Similarly, on the American continent, Loomis'
investigations show a mean depression of temperature 13°·9
C. below the average, the defect being greater the higher the
pressure, and markedly less near the Atlantic coast than in
inland regions.

The effects of strong radiation under anti-cyclonic conditions are also apparent in summer; the unusual power of
the sun's rays causes a great rise of temperature during the
day, and the heat thus received is freely parted with during
the night. The net result, at least in inland districts, is
simply to enormously increase the daily range; the heat
gained during the day is lost during the night, and hence
on the whole anti-cyclones are not associated with temperatures above the mean in summer—although the extra
quantity of heat received from the sun prevents the great
depression below the average which occurs in winter. In
the neighbourhood of the sea, as in north-western Europe and
on the Atlantic seaboard of America, summer anti-cyclones
are accompanied by higher mean temperatures, probably
because the nocturnal radiation is checked by the presence
of vapour brought in by the sea breeze during the day.

It must, of course, be borne in mind that we are here dealing
only with a thin stratum of the atmosphere in contact with
the surface of the earth. While the main body of the

atmosphere in an area of high pressure has its absorbing power reduced, this does not hold good close to the earth— where the air is not likely to contain less dust than usual, and where the supply of moisture is kept up from the ground or still more from the sea. This bottom layer may indeed be partly regarded as the body which absorbs and radiates heat. The lowering of temperature in it frequently leads to condensation, hence in fine summer weather valleys and low lying grounds are frequently enveloped in fog during the night, especially in the neighbourhood of lakes and streams where the supply of vapour is abundant. This cloud-covering serves to protect the earth's surface and vegetation growing on it; for when the deficiency of vapour is excessive even in the lowest layer of air the whole of the heat radiated is derived from the earth itself, and we find copious deposition of dew or even hoar frost, and growing plants are "nipped" or blackened when the air temperature is comparatively high. In insular and coast regions where the atmosphere never becomes very dry, or where the supply of rainfall is sufficient to ensure constant evaporation from the soil, these "ground frosts" are rather the exception than the rule, and never occur with great severity. It is obvious, however, that they are more likely to occur the greater the intensity of the anti-cyclonic system and the longer its duration, a matter of common experience in Britain, as appears from popular proverbs—*e.g.*, "Heavy dews in hot weather indicate a continuance of fair weather, and no dew after a hot day foretells rain." "If mists rise in low ground and soon vanish, expect fine weather."

"When the mist comes from the sea,
Then good weather it will be."

The low lying mists and fogs are in summer dissipated as the sun's rays gain power with the progress of the day, but in winter while the intensity of nocturnal radiation is greater the sun's heat is much less, and the mists frequently become permanent. Thus in Western Europe anti-cyclonic weather is in winter often characterized by cold wet mist or stratified cloud sometimes resting on the ground, sometimes rising a few hundred feet above it; all exposed objects are covered with ice-spicules condensed from the mist, which assume the most fantastic shapes, and the damp cold is extremely trying to all living creatures. Co-existing with these conditions we find in the upper atmosphere brilliantly clear weather with temperatures above the normal, and most intense dryness, characteristic of the true descending current.

These phenomena are familiar to anyone who has ascended a hill on a fine morning to see the sunrise. The sides of the hill up to a certain level are enveloped in thick mist, from which one suddenly emerges into a clear cloudless atmosphere—and if the peak be the highest in the neighbourhood no land may be visible from the summit, only a great undulating plain of cloud. After the dawn the cloud becomes tinged with red, and the colour grows rosier and warmer till the sun rises above the horizon and the whole expanse becomes dazzlingly bright. Then it slowly rises and disappears, to redescend in the cool of the evening.

71. *Temperature Gradient in Anti-Cyclones.*—From a scientific point of view the evidence obtained from high level observatories is still more striking. During winter anti-cyclones, when weather in plains and valleys is intensely cold, and, if there be enough vapour, misty and wet, temperature at mountain summits is far above the average for the time of year, and often above that at low levels, the sun shines with burning heat, and the drought is comparable to that of the deserts of Sahara or Arabia. Numerous examples of this have been discussed by Hann, Woeikof, [1] and others, comparing the records of observatories such as

[1] See *Met. Zeit.*, 1892, p. 361.

Santis, Pic du Midi, Puy de Dôme, etc., with corresponding observations at stations in plains and valleys; the most notable cases recorded are perhaps those of 23rd January to 3rd February 1876, and 20th and 30th December, 1879—of which the former was remarkable for mistiness and dampness, at low level, and the latter for intense cold. Similar conditions are also of common occurrence in the British Isles, as is shown by the records of the Ben Nevis Observatory.

The formation of ground fogs and low clouds in anti-cyclonic weather is a matter of vital importance to the farmer, since they serve to protect the surface of the ground from excessive cooling by nocturnal radiation. At certain seasons of the year warmth and sunshine are essential to the flowering or filling of grain crops, and these conditions are most fully realised in an area of high pressure. But if on account of long drought or other cause, the lower strata of the atmosphere are excessively deficient in aqueous vapour, saturation only occurs at extremely low temperatures, and radiation is not checked by the formation of cloud until vegetation is blighted by frost. Hence the most promising crops are often destroyed by ground-frost after a season of the finest weather, and the cause is often quite local, occurring most frequently in soils which do not retain moisture well. As an example of this we may quote the following sentence by Dr. Buchan, referring to Scotland : "On the night of August 31st to September 1st of 1885, the potato crop was totally destroyed, and grain crops in flower were also destroyed by frost in various localities in the valleys of Tweed, Nith, Clyde, and Spey. Over middle and upper Speyside, temperature on the ground fell to 15° F., with results most disastrous to these crops ; whereas at Dalnaspidal (1414 feet above the sea), in the district immediately contiguous, potatoes were scarcely, if at all blackened."[1] We may notice in this connection the familiar saying that

[1] *Trans. R. S. E.*, vol. xxxiv., p. xxiii.

when sheep go to the hill-tops at night the weather will be
fine, obviously because the nights are there drier and warmer
than in low lying ground.

72. *Föhn-winds.*—The peculiar phenomenon known as
Föhn-wind depends on principles analogous to those just
described. When a cyclone, or succession of cyclones,
follows a track in the neighbourhood of a range of mountains,
the air required for the supply of the ascending currents is
drawn from the slopes and valleys, creating a partial vacuum,
into which air from the higher levels descends as a hot dry
wind, sometimes of great violence. Since cyclones are in
general more frequent and more intense in the colder
months of the year, Föhn-winds occur oftenest in winter, and
since the lower strata of the atmosphere are relatively coldest
at that period the difference of temperature is most marked,
rising to 10° or 15° C. above the normal. The districts
most noted for these winds are the northern and southern
slopes of the Alps, the northern slopes of the Pyrenees,
the southern shores of the Caspian, the valley of the Missouri,
the southern island of New Zealand, and Greenland.

73. *Intermediate Systems.*—Since cyclones and anti-
cyclones are in general oval, it follows that between any
two such systems there must be an intermediate space, for
which we have not as yet fully accounted. We adhere to
our method of description from the distribution of pressure
or the shape of the isobars, and although no other system of
fundamental importance like the cyclone or anti-cyclone is
met with, these areas are of considerable practical consequence, inasmuch as they concern transition stages between
one great system and another. We accordingly find an unusually large number of sayings and prognostics relating to the
weather in these periods, especially where proximity of a
low pressure area is involved. These have been very fully
discussed for the British Islands by Abercromby,[1] and

[1] *Weather.* International Scientific Series. (Kegan Paul & Co.)

F

we shall confine ourselves chiefly to a summary of his results.

74. *Straight Line Isobars.*—Loomis remarks that between an area of high pressure and a neighbouring area of low pressure, the isobar of 30 inches, which may be taken to represent the average of pressure between the two systems, generally assumes the form of a straight line, and if these areas are much elongated, it may extend with little curvature for several thousand miles. We have, as a rule, a considerable area over which at least two or three straight isobaric lines (supposing them to be drawn for differences of 0·1 in. of pressure) are closely parallel to each other. In accordance with laws already known to us the wind at the earth's surface blows towards the lower pressure, making a nearly constant small angle with the isobars, but is usually fitful and gusty. On the outer limits of a straight isobar area, the weather has on the one side many characteristics of a cyclone, and on the other of an anti-cyclone; but between the two, in the straight isobar region proper, some peculiarities are observed, which probably depend on the fact that in the lower layers of the atmosphere warm air is being transferred from the anti-cyclone to the cyclone, and acquiring moisture from the earth by the way; and in the upper layers, cold air is moving in the opposite direction. Chief amongst these is the formation of very "hard"-looking stratified cloud, which sometimes entirely overcasts the sky, but is frequently broken by chinks through which the rays of the sun stream down, presenting the appearance known as "streamers" or "the sun drawing water." On account of vapour in the cloud strata it commonly happens, especially in winter, that chiefly red rays are transmitted through these openings, and the sky becomes wild and lurid. At the same time the atmosphere is very clear, distant objects are unusually distinct and well-defined, and the contrast of light and shadow unusually sharp. It seems likely that the

occurrence of these conditions in the early morning is the cause of the so-called " false dawn," recorded by observers from Omar Khyyam :—" Before the phantom of false morning died " to the negroes of North America, " If de sun git up berry early in de morning, and go to bed before he git up, it's a sign it rain before soon."

It must be distinctly understood, however, that we do not have any *sequence* of weather-changes, because an area of straight isobars cannot progress as a whole over a particular spot, except in the unheard of case of a cyclone and anti-cyclone moving in exactly the same direction, and with exactly the same speed. Lurid chinks, " streamers," " visibility," etc., associated with straight isobars, are prognostics of bad weather merely because of the proximity of a cyclone.

75. *Wedges.*—When two cyclones are close together a narrow wedge-shaped area of high pressure moves along between them in which the isobars are as represented in Fig. 19. One side of this is the rear of the retreating cyclone, and the other the front of the one following it ; hence in the former the barometer is everywhere rising, and in the latter falling, and the two are separated by a crest or wave-line, the *locus* of highest pressure. We may, so far as weather is concerned, regard the two flanks of the wedge as rear and front of cyclones, and the wedge itself as a projecting tongue of an anti-cyclone situated to one side.

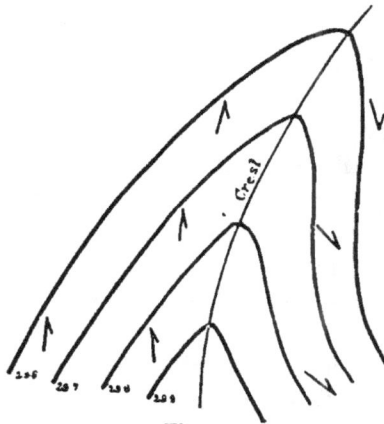

Fig. 19.

Observe that along the line of

the crest, where the barometer begins to fall again, the wind "jumps" or shifts suddenly to almost the opposite direction. Hence the saying, "A nor'-wester is not long in debt to a sou'-wester."

In the rear of the retreating cyclone we have the clearing up described in Chapter I. The atmosphere is, as in the straight isobars, unusually transparent, and distant objects look near. Hence the proverb, "The further the sight the nearer the rain," and Sir Patrick Spens'

> "I saw the new moon late yestreen,
>   Wi' the auld moon in her arm ;
> And if we gang to sea, master,
>   I fear we'll come to harm."

The central area is distinguished by the "radiation weather" described under anti-cyclones : but since the two depressions are always moving onward, the fine weather is only temporary, and is popularly described as "too fine to last," or "a pet day." The wide end of the wedge near the crest is often associated with fog, and the narrow end with thunderstorms or showers.

As the second depression approaches, the weather changes to that of a cyclone front—halo-bearing sky, restless animals, etc., but it is important to note the formation of the high cirrus clouds—revealing the out-flow from the south-east side of the cyclone towards the high pressure. These often take the form of stripes of fleecy cloud commonly called a "weather-head" or "Noah's Ark." In the British Isles, when the anti-cyclone lies well to the south, so that the depression moving eastward passes over the land, the weather-head will lie north-west to south-east ; but if the anti-cyclone extends well to the northward so that the depression skirting it is deflected to the north-east before reaching the coast, the axis of the wedge, instead of lying north and south, as in the first case, will be turned round towards west—and the weather-head will consequently extend in a north-east south-west direction. Hence with reference to "Noah's Ark" we find—

"North and south the sign of drought,
East and west the sign of blast."

and amongst Scottish fishermen the N.W.-S.E. and N.E.-S.W. directions are given.

76. *V-Shaped Depressions.*—The antithesis of wedge-shaped isobars occurs between two contiguous anti-cyclones in the form of a V-shaped depression, which again is of the nature of a tongue projecting from a cyclone situated to one side. On the advancing side of the V, with falling barometer, the weather is that of a cyclone front—halo-bearing sky, and increasing cloud, followed by a rain area which is bounded by the line of lowest pressure along the axis of the V, a line characterised by heavy squalls and clearing showers, as in the trough of a cyclone. The retreating side is simply the rear of a cyclone, detached clouds and then blue sky, with rising barometer. Along the line of the trough the wind "jumps" as in the wedge, suddenly reversing its direction.

77. *Line-Squalls and Secondaries.*—But V depressions are not necessarily bounded on each side by anti-cyclonic systems ; they are, as it were, a specialised form of cyclone or of part of a cyclone, and as such frequently occur within a cyclone of the ordinary or primary type. There is not, however, as in the former case, the same definition of form imposed ; hence the V sometimes becomes modified on the one hand into a long, narrow strip, or on the other into a smaller cyclone which is occasionally sufficiently developed to have a complete circulation, and is then called a

" secondary." The weather of such disturbances is to a certain extent that of the V first described, superposed upon that of the primary cyclone. The normal distribution of pressure in the latter may or may not be seriously altered as a whole, but gradients generally become steep and irregular, and in the immediate neighbourhood of the trough (which becomes the centre in a complete secondary) the wind usually blows in violent gusts, rain falls in torrents, accompanied by thunder and lightning—the last especially in summer, at which season these irregularities are most common.

In the attenuated or steep form the flanks of the V are greatly diminished, and the axis or trough becomes a kind of surge or wave, which is propagated at a speed varying within wide limits—one part sometimes moving with four times the velocity of another. Such belts are usually known as line-squalls or line-thunderstorms, and their energy is occasionally excessive. They give rise to a large proportion of the summer thunderstorms of Central Europe,[1] and are common in some parts of America, but comparatively rare in the British Isles, the most remarkable case amongst our records being that of 24th March, 1878, which struck and capsized H.M.S. *Eurydice.*

V-shaped depressions, secondaries, line-squalls, and thunderstorms are in general most erratic in all their movements, and their occurrence is, in consequence, excessively difficult to predict. The rapidity with which they sometimes travel, and the violence of rain, hail, or wind often developed within them, render them a source of great danger to life and property.

78. *Modifications Occurring in these Systems.*—We have now so far discussed the various forms of atmospheric movement depending upon the distribution of pressure, and have been able to connect with these most of the more important

[1] See Von Bezold, *Beob. d. Meteorol. Stat. in Kreiche. Bayern.* 1880.

phenomena of weather. We must, however, remember that the circulation in all the systems described up to this point, is determined by the deflecting force due to the rotation of the earth, acting according to Ferrel's law. It must be understood that, in describing these atmospheric movements, the average general path only is concerned, and that small local disturbances and eddies have not been considered. Thus, for example, if we state that in cyclones the direction of the wind makes a given angle with the isobars, we mean that the statement is true on the average of a large number of cases, and more nearly true for any one case the greater the intensity of the cyclone—for in a deep depression the forces due to the gradients are greater in proportion to local disturbing forces. In anti-cyclones, again, the gradients are, as a rule, so slight that large parts of the area are often distinguished by calms, or very light variable winds; but *on the whole* there is no doubt about the general circulation. For if we take a sufficiently large number of cases extending over a sufficiently large area—it is clear that local disturbances or distortions are just as likely to take place in one direction as in another, and hence they will, in the long run, balance each other, and leave the real circulation as the " most probable " result.

We are not at present concerned with the direct effects produced in special districts by the conformation of the earth's surface; these fall more properly under the heading of *Climate*, since their effect is constant; but we may briefly consider a few of the more important modifications which occur in the larger pressure systems.

79. *Squalls, Derechos.*—First comes the simple squall, which varies in intensity from the puff of wind whose progress is marked by "catspaws" on the surface of the sea, to the *Böen* of Germany, or the *derechos*,[1] the "straight blow of the prairies " of America. In their fully developed

---

[1] See Hinrichs, *Amer. Met. Jour.*, vol v., p. 306.

state, squalls are remarkable by the presence of a dense black cloud at no great elevation, which may be seen approaching — sometimes so quickly that it is impossible to shorten sail in the time between the first observation of the cloud on the horizon, and the ship being struck. The cloud, as seen from the advancing side, is in general of an arched form—hence the name "arched squall," and under the arch the wind blows in gusts, sometimes of great violence, and usually accompanied with deluges of rain, sleet, or hail, and much thunder and lightning. Within the squall pressure is greatly in excess, the barometer rising as much as 1 mm. or more, and falling again as the squall passes off. If the weather preceding the occurrence of the squall be warm and sunny, temperature usually suffers a sudden considerable fall—but if cloudy, little change is observed. Taking these facts together, and along with them the fact that the direction of wind in squalls is usually that of the lower cloud motion, there can be little doubt that squalls are caused by sudden downrushing of the air in the upper strata : and it seems probable that this is due to a sudden heavy fall of rain, bringing quantities of air down with it, simply by mechanical friction. The air thus brought down is dynamically warmed and dried, hence, in thunder showers of this type, it is not uncommon to find the air comparatively dry, even during a downpour of rain.

How the sudden excessive condensation arises is not so obvious, unless we accept the suggestion of Von Bezold, already referred to, that a mass of air may become supersaturated through the want of dust nuclei. Another explanation is afforded by supposing an extremely "stable" vertical gradient of temperature, such that cold, dense, upper layers of air break through lower warmer layers lying underneath, condensing the vapour in the latter, and causing them to ascend—thereby still further favouring the descent of cold air. It would seem that some process of this kind sometimes does take place without giving rise to condensation, as in the case of what are called "white squalls," which are occasionally sufficiently violent to dismast or even capsize vessels.[1] Captain Toynbee remarks that these squalls most frequently come from the direction of the upper current—thus at the northern limit of the S.E. trade winds, they often come from north-east, moving with the upper clouds, although the surface wind is S.E. or S. "White squalls" are not accompanied by rain or electrical disturbance—violent gusts occur suddenly without warning in fine weather.

This theory would also explain the squally, gusty winds characteristic of the trough and rear of eastward-moving cyclones; the sudden intrusion of cold polar winds over an area which has just experienced warm southerly or equatorial winds causing great condensation by the mixture of the two.

80. *Tornadoes.* — In contrast to the various kinds of squall attributable to a descent of upper currents, we have the sudden ascent, under similar conditions, of masses of warm air. This phenomenon, in its various degrees of intensity, gives rise to the familiar dust-whirls on a dry road, to the dust-storms and water-spouts of the tropics, and to the destructive tornado or "twister of the prairies." These whirlwinds are quite distinct from cyclones, inasmuch as their height greatly exceeds their diameter, and compared with cyclones, their diameter is extremely small; the smallest known cyclone extends over many times the area covered by the largest tornado, and there is no record of any phenomenon of an intermediate type. It is obvious that the rotation cannot therefore be due to the motion of the earth, and it is probably caused by accidental or local

[1] See Jahncke, *Q. J. Met. Soc.*, April, 1874.

deflection of the air in its movement towards the centre ; the "principle of equal areas," referred to in connection with cyclones, sufficiently explains how a very rapid rotation may be originated by a quite insignificant initial deflection, and it is easy to understand that air moving over the earth's surface is not likely to preserve an absolutely straight path for any length of time. Hence we find that in this class of disturbances, where an ascending current is involved, the rotational movement is a much more important element than in the squalls or "derechos" where the air has descended and escaped the rotational impulse due to surface irregularities. Indeed the increased wind-velocity in the squall is probably to a large extent simply the velocity of the upper current, which is normally greater than that of the under current, unimpeded by friction with the earth's surface.

The conditions of instability most favourable to the occurrence of whirlwinds differ to some extent from those most commonly associated with squalls. In the latter case it would seem that the process is chiefly mechanical, air being either dragged down by falling rain, or forcing itself down by its own inertia ; while in the former the action partakes more of the nature of a convection current. Hence squalls are most frequent where cold air is brought into contact with warm through the independent action of distribution of pressure, as in the trough and rear of a cyclone, but whirlwinds are most commonly experienced in the front of shallow depressions and during the warmest hours of the day, where there is little or no wind and the weather is sultry and oppressive. Thus we have in this country the well-known prognostic of dust-whirls preceding rain, and in the great tornado-regions of the United States the death-like stillness and silence is one of the surest precursors of these storms.

In this case, however, as in that of cyclones and anti-cyclones, the question of the cause of ascending and descending currents is one of great difficulty, and has not yet received an adequate answer.

Waterspouts are frequently seen on the Atlantic. A low cloud of great density is seen to bulge downwards on its lower side in the form of an inverted cone, and at the same time the surface of the sea underneath is thrown into violent commotion as if boiling. The conical cloud continues to descend, and the boiling sea appears to rise up to meet it, till the two columns join, and the spout appears suspended from the main body of the cloud above.

The apparent descent of the cloud in a waterspout is caused by the great reduction of pressure by centrifugal force within the whirling vortex, which allows the vapour inside the column to condense. When the rotation diminishes and the spout is about to break up, the pressure again increases, and the cloud evaporates, the column becoming transparent during the process. Waterspouts are usually succeeded by torrents of rain.

Dust or sand storms are of constant occurrence in the deserts of Africa and Arabia. They are simply spouts in which the waters of the sea are replaced by the sand of the desert. In the absence of either, the whirlwind becomes a tornado.[1]

The tornado is best known as the terrible scourge which devastates certain regions in the United States—notably Missouri, Kansas, and Georgia. It occurs at all times of the year, but most frequently in May ; and always in the southeast quadrant of an area of low pressure, generally at a distance of 300 to 500 miles from the centre. Preceded by a continuance of southerly winds and gradually increasing heat and moisture, or by a sultry oppressive atmosphere, the formation of the tornado begins with "the sudden appear-

[1] See Finley, *Report on Six Hundred Tornadoes* ; also *Amer. Met. Jour.*, vol. vii., (1890), p. 165

ance of ominous clouds, first in the south-west, then almost immediately in the north-west and north." "If the clouds are light, they resemble smoke rising from a burning building ; if dark, they present a deep greenish hue, which appears to increase in intensity as the storm advances. The motions of the clouds are peculiar, in that they appear to be rushing from every quarter towards a common centre, marking the incipient stages of a gyratory motion in the cloud region." Then follows the formation of the funnel-shaped cloud. The development of the storm is sometimes arrested here, and the only result is a severe hailstorm ; sometimes, again, it is confined to atmospheric layers at some elevation, and the tornado can be seen pursuing its course overhead with but little effect at the earth's surface : and even tornadoes which do reach the ground sometimes rise and redescend, leaving a track interrupted here and there by a series of breaks in which no damage is suffered.

Concerning tornadoes which do reach the ground, Finley states that the length of the path of destruction varies from 300 yards to about 200 miles, its average width being about 450 yards. The prevailing direction of progressive movement is north-east, with an average velocity of 44 miles an hour, which, however, varies within the wide limits 7 and 100. It would be easy to multiply harrowing descriptions of the destruction caused by these storms, of trees uplifted and driven down into the ground like stakes, of houses exploded by the air in their rooms expanding in the partial vacuum of the central whirl. But the final statements by Finley are sufficiently suggestive : "No structure that rises above the earth, however made, can wholly resist the violence of the tornado."—"No building can be made sufficiently large, strong, high, or low, or of any material whatever, to resist the force of the tornado's vortex." The approach of the tornado is accompanied by a noise resembling that of heavy machinery, which increases in intensity till the final

crash, which comes with the suddenness of an explosion.
The average duration of the storm at any one point is little
over a minute, but there is no way of escape except in " caves
and holes in the earth."

81. *Prediction of Squalls and Tornadoes.*—The special
prediction of squalls and whirlwinds is obviously, from the
nature of the case, an impossibility.   We can predict that a
given rock by the seashore will be covered by the tide on
certain days and at certain hours, but it is hopeless to predict how the advancing water will swirl and eddy round each
projecting angle or loose stone.   All that can be done is to
give due warning of the unstable state favourable to squalls
and whirls ; the rest must simply be watched for on the
spot.

CHAPTER V.

WEATHER FORECASTING.

82. *Methods of Forecasting*.—It will be understood from the facts outlined in the preceding chapters that the best method of predicting weather over any considerable extent of country is to study the general conditions of pressure, temperature, wind, etc., at a particular time, and then, by the help of past experience, to form a conjecture as to the changes most likely to follow. From what we know of the motions of cyclones and anti-cyclones, of their changes of form and intensity, the sudden development of secondaries and squalls, and so forth, and from our profound ignorance of the causes producing these changes, it is evident that anything like reliable prediction can only be attempted for a very short period. An expert forecaster can sometimes form a fairly accurate notion of the sequence of weather for two or three days in advance, but in practice it is found impossible to issue regularly anything like trustworthy predictions for much more than twenty-four hours. We may say that, given the synoptic chart representing the conditions over a certain area, say at 9 a.m. on a particular day, it is possible to predict what will be the general features of the chart till the same hour of the following day, with, under favourable conditions, a likelihood of being right five times out of six.

Under these circumstances, it is necessary for a forecasting service in any country that material for constructing a synoptic chart should be collected at a central office at least once daily, and since forecasts based on such charts are only valid for about twenty-four hours from the time at which the observations at the various stations are made, it is obvious that no time must be lost; for the time occupied in tabulating and reducing the observations, telegraphing the results to headquarters, plotting the data from all stations on the chart, drawing isobars, isothermals, etc., deducing the forecast from the indications of the chart and transmitting the forecast to the districts concerned, must all be deducted from the time for which the prediction holds good.

83. *Forecasting by Synoptic Charts.*—It is difficult, for obvious reasons, to lay down any hard and fast rules for predicting weather by means of charts. Experience alone can make a successful forecaster, and even the most expert cannot always assign full reasons for his predictions, so much is it a matter of simple judgment. We may, however, indicate a few general principles.

The first point to be looked at is the extent, form, and intensity of the regions of highest pressure. For, in the first place, where we find anti-cyclonic conditions, changes take place most slowly, and again, the high pressure areas to a great extent control the paths of the cyclones. By comparison with previous charts we can ascertain whether the anti-cyclones are extending and increasing in intensity, or retreating and breaking up. In the former case we can predict for the anti-cyclonic areas continued "radiation" weather, light winds, warm days, and dewy nights in summer, and cold or fog in winter; special attention being paid to the probability of ground-frosts likely to damage crops. In the latter case, we must observe carefully the breaking up of the high pressure system, noting the chances of its being penetrated by cyclones, and its effect on the cyclone tracks in its neighbourhood. Further, we must, when possible, determine the relations of the high pressure areas to the general circulation. Thus, for example, in Western Europe it is important to know when an anti-cyclone is a part of the

Atlantic high pressure system, or of the Eurasian, whether it is merely a ridge connecting the two, or a small system distinct from both. This is technically known as determining the *type* of weather, for it is found that the arrangements of the high pressure areas can be classified into a number of distinct types according to the relative extentand intensity of the different elements, and each of the great national weather offices employs a classification suitable to its special requirements.

The main features of the high pressure areas determined, the next point is to look for cyclones. These tend to follow certain routes in succession ; hence, by referring to former charts, we note the tracks of previous cyclones, and inquire whether, on account of alterations in the anti-cyclonic areas or other cause, we have any reason to expect that succeeding depressions will take a different path. In this connection we may make use of, for example, Van Bebber's cyclone tracks, or for the British Isles we may give weight to the fact that cyclone centres have a tendency to move up the English Channel, round the north-west coasts of Scotland and Ireland, along the line of the Caledonian Canal, or the Forth and Clyde Canal, or, more generally, that they select the line of least resistance. This done, we seek for signs of a cyclone actually approaching, reports of cirrus clouds, halos, sun-dogs, rising temperature, falling barometer, and so on ; and if we find any such, we obtain all possible data for forming an opinion as to its size, depth, position, direction of path, and rate of motion. This is, of course, the most important part of all forecasting, for we must ascertain whether the depression is of sufficient energy to merit the name of a storm, and the districts likely to be endangered must have timely warning. After its arrival, the cyclone must be carefully watched, and the districts over which it passes kept informed as to the changes of wind and weather corresponding to their position with respect to the centre. We must further determine whether the system is increasing in depth or filling up, and be on our guard against sudden changes of direction or speed, which would falsify predictions and leave certain coasts unwarned. Again, a constant look-out must be kept, especially during the passage of shallow depressions in the warmer months of the year, for the formation of V depressions or secondaries, or rather for conditions favourable to their development. This is at once the most difficult and one of the most important points to be attended to in order that some warning may be given of squalls or severe hail and thunder storms.

As the cyclone passes off, we look carefully for indications of another following it, a check in the fall of temperature accompanying the rear, the unusual clearness, "refraction," or radiation characterising a "pet" day, the reappearance of cirrus clouds, or a check in the rise of the barometer, with a backing wind. Here the British Isles stand at a very great disadvantage in the matter of forecasting, for cyclones almost invariably approach from the westward, and travel with considerable velocity. But immediately to the west is the Atlantic, from which we obtain no sign—the first notice we can receive of an approaching storm is from Valentia, only 400 miles west of London ; hence a rapidly moving storm may be upon us almost before it is possible to give warning.

84. *Storm Warnings.*—The work of storm warning is in practice to a great extent distinct from that of ordinary continuous forecasting. In the British Meteorological Office, on the approach of a cyclone of dangerous intensity, special messages are sent out warning the coasts likely to be affected. The warnings thus received are made public by the exhibition of certain signals. In this country these take the form of a cone, which is hoisted at seaports on receipt of the warning message. When hoisted with its apex downwards, the

cone signifies that strong winds may be expected, at first

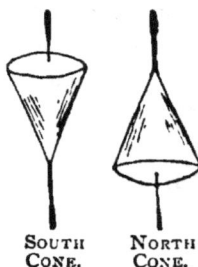

SOUTH
CONE.   NORTH
CONE.

Fig. 20.

from southward or south - westward. Hoisted apex upwards, it means that strong winds from northward or north-eastward may be expected. These signals are at best merely a caution of the most general kind, and further details of the approaching disturbance must be obtained from the warning telegram itself, which is (or ought to be) always posted up for public inspection.

The student who has fairly mastered the contents of the preceding chapters will find a study of the Daily Weather Reports of the Meteorological Office, or of the Deutsche Seewarte, the most profitable meteorological exercise to which he can address himself. Let him take a chart for a given day, and after comparing it with those for say a week previous, attempt a forecast for the twenty-four hours following ; after which let him compare his forecast with that issued by the office, and both with the report of actual weather issued the following day. Where either or both of the forecasts is found to have failed, let him carefully inquire in what the failure principally consists—temperature, wind, rain, etc., and seek for hints to be useful in future.[1]

85. *Forecasting for Isolated Observers.*—We have seen that the forecaster at a central station labours under great disadvantages from the unavoidable incompleteness of

[1] The British Daily Weather Reports may be obtained from the Secretary, Meteorological Office, 63 Victoria Street, S.W., London, post free as issued for £1 per annum. For further practical information in forecasting see Abercromby, *Weather*, International Scientific Series, 1887, or *Principles of Weather Forecasting* also by Abercromby, published by the Meteorological Council (Stanford, 1885). Also R. H. Scott, *Weather Charts and Storm Warnings*, 3rd edition, Longmans, 1887.

the data from which he has to work ; and that at best his predictions can only be of the most general character.   But on
the other hand the practical man, who wants to foretell the
weather at the particular station at which he lives and moves,
labours under the disadvantage of not being able to get the
general view afforded by the synoptic chart.   Hence the
sailor on board ship, and the fisherman or farmer in remote
districts, must depend wholly on his own observations to
furnish him with the means of prediction.   We propose now
to give some hints which may be helpful in applying the
principles already explained, premising again that nothing
can replace long and careful observation—many an old salt
blissfully ignorant of all scientific meteorology is nevertheless
a practical forecaster of the greatest proficiency.

First, and most important, we have for the northern hemisphere Buys Ballot's rule, for enabling us to form a notion
of the distribution of pressure :—

"Stand with your back to the wind, and the centre of
lowest pressure lies about two points in advance of your left
hand."

We shall not in general find much difficulty in recognising
anti-cyclonic weather—the high barometer, the direction and
force of wind, and the " radiation " effects described by so
many prognostics, are unmistakable.   It is then only necessary to keep a strict watch on the progress of an anti-cyclone,
so as not to miss the first signs of its breaking up.   During
a spell of fine weather the barometer rises, perhaps a little
irregularly, but on the whole steadily, till a maximum is
reached, after which it begins to fall again slowly ; showing
that the anti-cyclone is either retreating or breaking up.
This gradual dissolution may go on for days, with little
change in the weather beyond a slightly increased cloudiness,
but the first indications of an approaching cyclone must be
looked for, a sudden increase in the rate at which the
mercury falls—any of the signs of increased humidity de-

scribed in the prognostics—or the appearance of "mares' tails," or windy cirrus clouds; the direction and rate of motion of these last being of great importance. Cirrus moving rapidly from west or north-west may be accepted, in Britain at least, as a very reliable warning.

After satisfying ourselves in various ways that a cyclone is actually approaching, the next step is to find the position of its centre, its direction and rate of motion, and its extent. This can usually be done with a fair approximation to accuracy by a careful study of the changes of the wind, with the help of Buys Ballot's Law and constant observation of the barometer; a close watch being kept all the time on the appearance of the sky. We note that when the barometer falls rapidly and the direction of wind does not change, we may expect the centre to pass directly over us; when the barometer falls rapidly and the wind veers quickly, we are near the path of the centre, of a deep depression if the winds are violent, and of a rapidly moving one if they are only of moderate strength; and when the barometric fall is gradual and the change of wind direction is slow, we are at a considerable distance from the path of the centre, the wind again veering faster the faster the depression is travelling.

The next change to be looked for is the passage of the line of the trough—marked by the barometer rising again—after which, of course, we may predict the weather characteristic of the rear of a cyclone. Observe, however, that all these rules for a single isolated station may be greatly modified by a cyclone of elongated form; the changes at the two ends are then very sudden, and very gradual in the intermediate parts.

As before, the tendency of cyclones to follow each other in succession must be kept in mind, and after one passes off the conditions associated with a "wedge" or "straight isobar" must be examined for the smallest indications of another depression.

It is unnecessary to go into further detail, which would simply involve repetition of much that has been already explained. We may simply give as general cautions :—

(1). Although cyclones occur most frequently when barometric pressure is low generally, and the converse, the *changes* from time to time are the most important factors to be observed. The words " rain," " change," " fair," engraved on the barometer are always misleading, and altogether wrong when the instrument is used at any place other than that at which it was constructed, on account of the change of level.

(2). In general the rule

> " Long foretold, long last,
> Short notice, soon past,"

holds good.

(3). A southerly wind is much more likely to veer to the northward with the sun than a northerly to the southward.

(4). All the ordinary interpretations of barometric indications, sky appearances, wind changes, etc., are liable at any time, but especially in summer, to be falsified by a sudden change of course in a cyclone, or by squalls, secondaries, V depressions and such disturbances.

A good deal of help may often be obtained from *local* prognostics. On the west coast of Ireland and Scotland a heavy ground swell or breaking surf is accounted a sure precursor of a storm, because the sea disturbance occasioned by a cyclone frequently outstrips the cyclone itself. Again, we have innumerable local prognostics depending on humidity, visibility, etc. In Lancashire, we find the saying,

> " If Riving Pike do wear a hood,
> Be sure the day will ne'er be good ; "

and at Plymouth, if from the Hoe the Breakwater light (2 miles distant) and the Eddystone light (14 miles distant) seem of the same colour or brightness, it is a sign of rain next day.

The most successful forecasting may, of course, be accomplished by combining local observation with a study of synoptic charts. The knowledge of general conditions derived from the latter can then be modified to suit local peculiarities. We know, as it were, what to look out for, and can at once recognise the earlier stages of the different changes.

CHAPTER VI.

METEOROLOGICAL INSTRUMENTS AND OBSERVATIONS.

86. *Need for more Accurate Measurements.* — We have found that, as stated at the outset, it is possible to observe many of the meteorological elements with sufficient accuracy for describing weather changes, without the aid of instruments. Up to this point, we have employed only the barometer to measure changes of pressure otherwise imperceptible, and the thermometer to enable us to distinguish temperature effects from those of moisture.

But when, instead of the main characteristics of change from day to day, we come to consider the average result of all the variations from month to month and year to year, to compare the weather of say, one summer with that of another or with the average of a long succession of summers, or to contrast the average weather of different places during the same periods, then these methods become inadequate. We must increase the accuracy of our observations, and by instrumental or other aids transform them into quantitative measurements which can be compared amongst themselves, and subjected generally to the ordinary methods of mathematical treatment.

The making of meteorological observations presents for the most part no great difficulty—the essential qualification is merely a capacity for doing a small piece of routine work at stated times without losing interest in it, and so becoming careless.

87. *Observations must be Comparable.*—In observational work connected with climatology one point must always be kept in view—that the principal value of the records consists in their bearings on those of neighbouring stations. The first essential, therefore, is that the observations at different

places must be *comparable*, the instruments used must be similar in form, and must be exposed in a similar way, and the errors peculiar to them and to the observer must be known. Thus in some cases it is not advisable to use the best known instrument for observing a certain phenomenon, because although some observers may have skill to use it, many may not, and the few sets of more accurate observations are not comparable with those made at the majority of stations. We shall confine ourselves to describing instruments and methods in general use in this country, and we may state generally that *all* instruments should have their errors of construction determined by comparison with the recognised standards at Kew Observatory.

88. *Observations of Air Temperature.*—We have already discussed the variations of air temperature with some detail, and are therefore in a position to understand the nature of the quantitative measurements required. These are, in general, the mean daily temperature and the daily extremes. The latter are measured by self-registering maximum and minimum thermometers, and the former either by averaging a number of observations at fixed hours, or by applying a correction to the mean of the maximum and minimum. (See § 35.)

Now, it must be remembered that with the exception of pressures, meteorological observations are not measurements of precision like, for example, electrical measurements. In determining air temperatures or humidities or the direction and force of winds, we are not concerned to make measurements of great accuracy which refer only to the air in the immediate neighbourhood of the instruments at the moment of observation. What we want is a fairly correct estimate of the general conditions.

Take one example. If we observe air temperatures with a thermometer of great sensitiveness, fully protected from radiation effects by a silvered thimble on the bulb, we shall find constant variations from minute to minute, sometimes amounting to a degree or more, whether the air is calm or not.[1]   Hence it appears that there are incessant local variations, and in order to get the average temperature near a given station, say at 9 a.m., we should take readings every minute from say five minutes before the hour till five minutes past, and find the mean.   But in practice this is much more easily done by using a less delicate thermometer, which, as it were, averages the small variations for itself, and gives the result of all the minute rises and falls of temperature to which it is exposed.

89. *The Thermometer.*—The thermometer most usually employed has a spherical bulb $\frac{1}{4}$ to $\frac{3}{8}$ inch in diameter, although some observers prefer a cylindrical form ; and its accuracy is tested to $0°·1$ (F. or C.).   Note that whatever be the form of the attached scale—which may be of wood, porcelain, or zinc—the degrees *must* be engraved on the stem, otherwise we have no guarantee that the zero points do not shift.   The scale most commonly used in this country and in America is that of Fahrenheit, of which the chief merits are that it does not involve the use of minus quantities for temperatures below freezing, and that the degrees are of convenient length.   On the other hand, it has the disadvantage of requiring to be converted into the centigrade scale whenever any theoretical investigations or comparisons with Continental work are involved.   The matter is, however, unimportant, as the difficulties presented by the conversion are not formidable.   This and all other meteorological computations are best performed by means of tables, to be found in the official *Instructions in the Use of Meteorological Instruments* of the Meteorological Office, or Hazen's *Tables*, or the somewhat bulky edition of Guyot's *Tables* issued by the Smithsonian Institution.

90. *Reading the Thermometer.*—In reading a thermometer

[1] Aitken, *Proc. R. S. E.*, xii., p. 687.

the principal error to be guarded against is that due to parallax, or not having the eye directly opposite the point at which the liquid stands. When the liquid in question is mercury, this is easily avoided by making the degree mark on the stem coincide with its reflection in the mercury column.

The limit of accuracy required in the readings is one-tenth of a degree (0°·1). The marks on the stem usually represent whole degrees, and the tenths are obtained by estimating the position of the top of the column with reference to the degrees above and below. It may be remarked that the *five* degree marks, and frequently the freezing-point mark, are longer than the others, and care must be taken in determining the whole degrees of the reading not to confuse these longer marks with each other. The most careful observer will sometimes record 42° or 34° for 37°; he sees that the reading is 2° above a long mark, and mistakes the 35° mark for 32° or 40°, and so on.

91. *Self-registering Thermometers.*—The forms of self-registering thermometers are numerous. We refer the reader to larger treatises for detailed descriptions. The *maximum* thermometer most usually employed is that of Phillips, which is merely an "ordinary" mercurial thermometer with its stem placed horizontally, and the mercury column broken by a small bubble of air.

The *minimum* thermometer in almost universal use was devised by Rutherford in 1794. The liquid employed is alcohol, and in the alcohol column is placed a small glass index.

92. *Thermometer Exposure.*—The proper exposure of thermometers so that they may indicate the true temperature of the air is a matter of great difficulty. The conditions required are two—a constant circulation must be kept up round the thermometer bulbs, and in its passage to the instruments the air must not have its temperature changed by passing over hot or cold surfaces, and the thermometer bulbs must be protected not only from the direct rays of

the sun, but from radiations of all kinds from surrounding objects. These conditions are probably most nearly realised by the sling thermometer, which is attached to a cord some two feet in length and swung round like a sling, the operation being of course performed in the shade. There are,

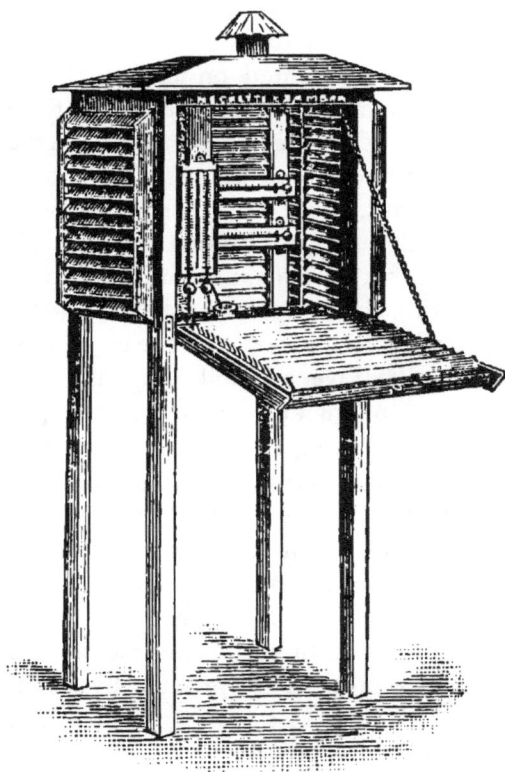

Fig. 21.

however, many objections to observations of this kind, and various forms of thermometer shelter have been devised, none of them altogether satisfactory. That used in this country is called after its inventor the "Stevenson" screen, and except perhaps on unusually calm hot days gives fairly accurate results. It consists merely of a wooden box, as shown in Fig. 21, the sides of which are composed of a double row of louvre boards placed opposite ways. The top is solid and the bottom entirely open.

The screen should be placed on a level grass plot of considerable extent, and well clear of buildings, trees, rising ground, or anything likely to interfere with free circulation of air. It should be mounted on legs so that the bulb of the ordinary thermometer is just 4 feet from the ground.

93. *Calculation of Mean Temperature.*—As already explained, if we accept the average of twenty-four hourly observations of temperature as the true mean for the day, we can obtain a close approximation to this value for any given day without actually making the hourly observations, either by observing the temperature at suitable hours, or by applying a proper correction to the mean of the maximum and minimum. We give the following hours as affording the best averages—9 a.m. and 9 p.m. ; 10 a.m. and 10 p.m. ; 3 a.m. and 3 p.m. ; 6 a.m., 2 p.m., and 10 p.m. ; any four hourly intervals. The mean of maximum and minimum may be taken as about $0°\cdot5$ F. above the average temperature for nearly all climates, but more accurate results may be obtained for the British Isles by employing the following method. "Multiply[1] the difference between the observed maximum and minimum by the proper factor obtained from the following table, and add the product to the minimum "

Month.			Factor.
January and December,	.	.	$0\cdot520$
February and November,	.	.	$0\cdot500$
March and October,	.	.	$0\cdot485$
April and September,	.	.	$0\cdot476$
May and August, .	.	.	$0\cdot470$
June and July,	.	.	$0\cdot465$

94. *Accumulated Temperature.*—We shall have occasion later on to make use of another quantity deduced from

[1] *Weekly Weather Report,* 1881, p. 3.

temperature observations—the *accumulated* temperature. It has been found that when the air is warmer than a certain neutral temperature, the progress of vegetation is accelerated, and hence it becomes important, having fixed that point, to know how much and for how long the temperature is above or below it.   The investigations of A. de Candolle have shown that in the case of most plants vegetation does not actively commence till a temperature of somewhere about 6° C. or 42° F. is reached, and this temperature is therefore accepted as the base.   But now there arises the difficulty of computing in a convenient way the amount of heat at a temperature above 42° F., received by a plant.   We want a means of expressing the amount by which the temperature exceeded 42° F., and the time it continued above that point.

This problem has been solved by General Strachey's conception of a "day-degree."   One day-degree is a difference of 1° F. from the base temperature continued for 24 hours. Thus an average temperature of 43° F. for 24 hours means one day-degree positive, or to the good for vegetation; an average of 41° for the same period means one day-degree negative, or lost.   Hence for each kind of crop we can begin at seed-time, add all the positive day-degrees, omit all the negative, and estimate the total required to ripen the crop.

We are at present only concerned with the practical question of calculating the number of day-degrees for a given period.   The following rules are taken from the Weekly Weather Report for 1884:—

Rules for computing for a Weekly Period the Accumulated Temperature above or below 42° F. from the observed Maximum and Minimum.

1. Obtain the mean temperature, from the means of the seven observed maxima and minima, in the manner already described for daily values.   (§ 93.)

2. In obtaining the accumulated temperature four cases may occur, to which the following rules will apply :—

Conditions of Temperature.	To obtain the Accumulated Temperature.	
	Above 42° F.	Below 42° F.
If the minimum is *above* 42° F. or *equal* to 42° F.	Subtract 42° F. from the mean.	There is none.
If the minimum is *below* 42° F., but the mean *above* 42° F.	From the difference between the mean for the day and the maximum, deduct the accumulated temperature below 42° F., calculated as stated in the next column.	The required quantity is the excess of 42° F. over the minimum, multiplied by the coefficient 0'4.
If the mean is *below* 42° F., but the maximum *above* 42° F.	The required quantity is the excess of the maximum over 42° F., multiplied by the coefficient 0'4.	From the difference between the mean for the day and the minimum, deduct the accumulated temperature above 42° F., calculated as stated in the preceding column.
If the maximum is *below* 42° F., or *equal* to 42° F.	There is none.	Subtract the mean from 42° F.

This gives the average daily temperatures for the week in each case, and must be multiplied by 7 to give the totals for the week.

As an example—let the mean of seven maxima for a week in February be 47°·3 and of the corresponding minima 34·6 : then the mean for the week is 41°·0.   By third line in the table, day-degrees above 42° F.

$$= (47·3 - 42·0) \times 0·4 = 2·1 \text{ average per day ;}$$

and below 42° F.

$$= (41·0 - 34·6) - 2·1 = 4·3 \text{ average per day.}$$

Hence for the week we have

Day-degrees to the good $= 2·1 \times 7 = 14·7$

,,   lost $= 4·3 \times 7 = 30·1.$

Collecting these figures week by week, we get a kind of debit and credit account as the season advances.

95. *Temperature of Radiation.*—Radiation thermometers are commonly employed to afford a measure of the intensity of the heat radiations received from the sun or given off by the surface of the earth.

The *black bulb* thermometer is an ordinary maximum having the bulb covered with lamp black, a substance which absorbs practically all heat rays falling upon it, and enclosed in a glass jacket, which is exhausted of air and hermetically sealed.   When freely exposed to the action of the sun's rays the thermometer rises until the heat received by the bulb in unit time is just equal to that lost by radiation to the enclosing jacket, which latter remains approximately at the temperature of the air.   The maximum recorded by the black bulb *minus* the maximum temperature of the air is taken as a measure of the maximum heating intensity of the sun's rays for the day.

It cannot, however, be said that the indications of the black bulb thermometer are of much value.   In the first place the sun's rays do not in general attain their greatest power at the hour of maximum air temperature, but

considerably earlier, and we should therefore subtract from
the black bulb reading not the maximum, but the actual
air temperature at the time the black bulb reaches its
highest point.   Again, it is almost impossible to construct instruments exactly alike in the covering of the
bulb, the formation of the jacket, and the amount of the exhaustion.   Finally, supposing the instrument perfectly adapted
to its purpose, it is doubtful if the data afforded by it would
be of much value.   Here again, what is really wanted is a
measure of total heat received, not of maximum intensity at any
instant.   The actinometers of Pouillet, Crova, Langley, and
others, which to a certain extent give this, are, unfortunately,
not suited for general use; but much may be learned from the
duration of direct solar radiation, even without attempting to
estimate its intensity.

96. *Sunshine.*—This is measured by means of sunshine recorders, of which various forms have recently
been devised, that known as the Campbell-Stokes, in which
the sun's rays are concentrated by means of a glass ball and
made to leave a charred record on a strip of prepared paper,
being probably the most reliable.

97. *Terrestrial Radiation.*—The terrestrial radiation
thermometer is an extremely sensitive Rutherford minimum.
The bulb is modified so as to present the greatest amount
of surface relatively to its contents, either by making it in
the form of a hollow cylinder, or by drawing it out and
bending it back upon itself.   The instrument is exposed on
a surface of close short grass, being supported upon two
forked sticks so that the bulb just touches the tips of the
blades.

If we grant, what is extremely doubtful, that the reading
of this thermometer really represents the lowest temperature
reached by the surface of the grass during the night, it is
obvious that we have not gained much information, for that
temperature does not depend on radiation alone, but on the

temperature and moisture of the soil underneath, and on the length and closeness of the grass ; and hence not only the readings at different places, but even those at the same place on different nights are not comparable. Still, the method has a certain value, inasmuch as by subtracting the minimum on grass from the minimum temperature of the air we get a rough estimate of nocturnal radiation, which may be useful in agricultural matters.

98. *The Barometer.*—Since the strictly local variations of pressure in the atmosphere are, for the most part, extremely small, the barometer in its application to meteorology may be accurately called an instrument of precision. It consists essentially of two parts—the glass tube containing the mercurial column and the scale for measuring the length of that column.

The only corrections which must be applied to the height of the mercurial column are due (1) to capillarity, and (2) to change of density in the mercury. Since mercury does not *wet* the interior of the tube, the capillary forces always depress the column, making it shorter than it would otherwise be by an amount which is greater the smaller the tube. Hence also the mercury surface in the tube is convex upwards, and we measure the column from the central summit —*not* from the point of contact with the glass. Again, the density of mercury depends upon its temperature, and the less the density the longer will be the column necessary to balance the pressure of the air. It is usual to accept the density of pure mercury at 32° F. as a standard, and to reduce all observations of the barometer to that temperature. Both of these corrections are in practice included with others referring to the scale, so we need not discuss them further at present.

The scale, which must be made of brass if the observations are to yield results of scientific value, is (except where extreme accuracy is required) engraved on a tube which

H

forms the case of the instrument. Any error in its construction must be ascertained by comparison with a standard. Now, we must clearly understand what exactly is the quantity we want to measure. Observe that the mercurial column may be of any *length;* we may fill the whole tube, however long, by inclining it. The pressure is not measured by the length, but by the vertical distance between the top of the mercury in the tube and the surface of it in the cistern.

Hence—

(1) The scale must be exactly vertical. This is easily arranged by allowing the barometer to swing freely, either by a hook or on gimbals.

(2) Since when the mercury column falls some mercury flows out of the tube into the cistern, and when it rises out of the cistern into the tube, the level of the mercury surface in the cistern varies with every change of pressure, and some means must be adopted of adjusting either the zero end of the scale to the mercury surface, or the mercury surface to the zero end of the scale ; or else of making proper allowance for the error introduced in the absence of such adjustment.

A modified application of the first method is the *siphon* barometer much used on the Continent. The "cistern" proper is done away with, and the lower end of the tube bent through two right angles, so as to form a siphon. The positions of the mercury in both legs of the siphon are then measured, and the difference of level gives the height of the barometer.

The second method, of adjusting the mercury surface to the zero point of the scale, was first applied in practical form by Fortin, and is now generally used in the better class of instruments. The bottom of the cistern is made of a flexible material such as leather, and is kept in position by an external piston. The piston can be moved by means of a screw, and the surface of the mercury in the cistern raised and lowered at will. The zero point of the scale is usually an ivory index to which the mercury is adjusted either directly or by a float the stem of which bears a mark corresponding to one on the index.

In the third class of instruments, where no special adjustment is made, the zero of the scale is placed at a neutral point, and a " capacity correction " is applied to all readings above or below that point. The amount of this correction is sometimes marked on the instrument, but more usually incorporated in the scale, which is then divided into inches (or millimetres as the case may be) *plus* or *minus* the capacity correction.

(3) Since the length of the scale varies with temperature all measurements made with it must be accompanied by a statement of the temperature of the instrument at the time of observation, so that they may be reduced to a standard temperature at which the scale is correct. It is usual to combine this correction with the temperature correction required for the mercury column, and to express the joint result in a table for reducing barometric observations to 32° F. Observe that except in special cases these tables refer to barometers with *brass* scales.

The temperature of the instrument is determined by means of an "attached thermometer," the bulb of which is placed inside the brass case. In making an observation this should be read first, and the barometer should always be hung where sudden great changes of temperature do not occur—so that both mercury column and brass scale shall be at a fairly uniform temperature throughout.

At the upper end of the scale the brass tube forming the case has two slits cut in opposite sides of it, exposing the barometer tube inside and enabling us to observe the rise and fall of the mercury. In the slits two small brass slides are placed, with their lower edges in exactly the same horizontal plane ; these slides can be moved up and down by a rack and pinion arrangement, and the plane of their lower

edges marks the level to be measured by the scale. Hence to
" set " the barometer, we bring the lower edges of the two
slides into an exact straight line with the highest point of
the mercury in the centre of the tube. Fig. 22 represents a
section through the tube, A A the two slides. In making
the adjustment it is necessary to have a strong light behind

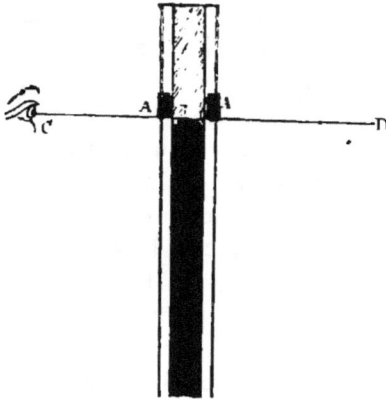

Fig. 22.

the instrument, so as to be
able to see when the ray
C D is just cut off by
the top of the mercury B
and the slides.

Having set the slides
in position we have next
to obtain the reading on
the scale, which we may
repeat is the distance between the ivory zero or
the " neutral point " as
the case may be, and the
lower edge of the slide.

99. *The Vernier.*—The degree of accuracy usually required is one five-hundredth (·002) of an inch, and in order
to distinguish so small divisions, we employ the device in-
vented by Peter Vernier in (*ca*) 1630, and known by his name.

Along the side of one slit is engraved the *fixed* scale of
inches divided into tenths (·100) and half-tenths (·050).
The vernier or *movable* scale is screwed to the slide which
moves in the same slit, and its zero coincides with the lower
edge, the point to be measured. The whole length of the
vernier corresponds to twenty-four divisions of the fixed
scale, *i.e.* twenty-four half-tenths $(24 \times ·050 = 1·200)$, and
that length is on it divided into a number of parts greater
by one—twenty-five ; hence one division of the vernier is
equal to $\frac{1}{25} \times 1·200 = ·048$ or one five-hundredth of an inch
(·002) less than one division of the fixed scale.

If, then, the zero line of the vernier is at the same level as (say) the line of 29·000 inches on the fixed scale, so that these two appear as one straight line, then the *first* division of the vernier will be ·002 inch below the first of the fixed scale, the *second* ·004 inch below the second, and so on ; and therefore conversely if the first line of the vernier corresponds with the first of the fixed scale, then the zero of the vernier must be ·002 above the line of 29·000 inches on the fixed scale. But the zero of the vernier is the point we wish to measure, hence the reading is 29·000 inches + ·002 inches = 29·002. Similarly, if the second line of the vernier corresponds to the second of the fixed scale, the zero of the vernier is ·004 above the 29·000 inches line, and the reading is 29·004 inches, and so on. Hence, generally, having set the slide :—

(1) Note the division on the fixed scale which comes next *below* the zero point of the vernier.

(2) Starting from the zero point of the vernier, count the divisions *upwards* till that one is reached which is in correspondence with any line on the fixed scale. Multiply the resulting number by ·002, and add the product to (1). The sum is the reading required.   •

In practice, every fifth line on the vernier, which, of course, marks one hundredth of an inch (5 × ·002 = ·010) bears a figure, and the intermediate lines obviously mark ·002, ·004, ·006, ·008 respectively ; hence, after ascertaining which line corresponds to one on the fixed scale, we may read off directly, obtaining the hundredths from the first figure below the line so found, and the five-hundredths by allowing ·002 for each intermediate line on the vernier. This avoids the counting and multiplication of (2) above.

100. *Summary of Reductions in Reading Barometer.—* We may summarise the steps in observing the pressure at the cistern of the barometer as follows :—

(*a*) Read attached thermometer.

(*b*) Adjust mercury in cistern to zero point of scale, if the instrument is constructed on Fortin's principle.

(*c*) Set and read vernier.

(*d*) Apply capacity correction where adjustment (*b*) cannot be made.

(*e*) Apply Kew correction for scale error and capillarity.

(*f*) Reduce result of foregoing to standard temperature, 32° F.

These are necessary and sufficient for making all observations at exactly the same place comparable with each other, and we may remark in passing that pressure observations should be published in this form, without further reduction.

101. *Reduction to Sea-Level.*—When we come to compare the readings of the barometer at one station with simultaneous readings at another, a correction for difference of level in the two instruments must be applied. The most convenient method for general use is to reduce the observations at *all* stations to sea-level ; and it is therefore most important that the height of the barometer cistern above mean sea-level should be accurately known. It is not too much to say that the value of barometer observations for scientific purposes largely depends on accuracy in this matter. The height being known we reduce to sea-level by applying the formula of § 49. Observe that this involves the assumption of certain stable conditions, and also a knowledge of the vertical temperature gradient, and that in consequence it is not always accurate.

102. *Calculation of Mean Pressure.*—From what has been said in § 36 it will be understood that the reduction of barometer observations taken at any hour, or set of hours, to the true daily mean is by no means so simple a matter as in the case of temperature observations. The great variations in different seasons and at different places both

in the form and amplitude of the phases of the curves make it impossible to give a general rule for the correction for daily range. For special inquiries in which the records of a large number of stations in different parts of the globe have to be compared, involving observations at different sets of hours, corrections calculated from the hourly observations of some standard station having a similar climate are applied to each individual case ; but great care must be exercised in selecting the standard for comparison. We must not, for example, employ the data of a station having an insular climate to correct observations from one situated in a continental region, for the daily curves of the two may be almost exactly opposite in form. The following table, calculated from data given by Buchan,[1] shows the average corrections to be applied to the means of observations at 9 a.m. and 9 p.m., 6 a.m., 2 p.m., and 10 p.m., and 9 a.m., 3 p.m., and 9 p.m. at a number of typical stations in order to reduce them to the true mean of the day. They refer only to the whole year, and in most cases vary considerably from month to month :—

| | | Corrections to be applied to mean of observations at (thousandths of an inch). | | |
		Hours. 9 : 9	Hours. 6 : 2 : 10	Hours. 9 : 3 : 9
Atlantic Ocean,	{ Lat. 5°-10° N., Long. 20°-30° W., }	− 30	0	− 9
	Valentia,	− 5	0	− 3
	Kew,	− 9	+ 1	− 2
	Culloden,	− 5	0	− 1
	Ben Nevis Observatory,	− 3	0	− 3
	Gries,	− 16	− 1	+ 4
	Pola,	− 6	+ 1	− 2
	Moscow,	− 2	0	0
	Batavia,	− 36	− 1	− 4
	Sitka,	0	0	0

We note that the average of observations at 6 a.m., 2 p.m.,

[1] *Challenger Reports*, "Atmospheric Circulation," p. 13.

and 10 p.m. gives a close approximation to the true mean in all the widely different cases included in the table ; hence this makes an excellent combination of hours for barometric observations. The correction to be applied to the average of 9 a.m. and 9 p.m. varies between the limits ·000 at Sitka, and − ·036 at Batavia, being greatest for what we may call oceanic climates, and least in insular climates or places situated on the western confines of a continental area, where the "morning maximum" is delayed. In the British Isles the correction for these hours varies between − ·005 at Valentia, and − ·009 at Oxford and Greenwich, averaging about − ·006 over all.

103. *Non-Mercurial Barometers.*—It is unnecessary to give here any description of the various delicate pressure gauges used as barometers. The aneroid, metallic barometer, etc., while undoubtedly of great value for many purposes, cannot replace the mercurial barometer for regular observations, not because their errors are large, but because they are variable. Observations with the best of aneroids must be constantly checked by comparison with those of a mercurial barometer.

Special mention must, however, be made of *self-recording* barometers and thermometers. The most accurate instruments, which continuously record their readings by means of photography, are only suitable for specially equipped observatories, but in recent years cheap barographs and thermographs have been introduced, notably by Richard Frères of Paris. These instruments, particularly the barograph, give tracings which are extremely valuable when combined with the ordinary eye-observations. Using two daily readings of the mercurial barometer to determine the error of the barograph, the latter can be made to yield data sufficiently accurate for the determination of the diurnal barometric curve, besides affording a great deal of information about changes of pressure generally, and on the other hand the automatic records afford a ready means of detecting errors in the eye-observations.

104. *Wind Observations: Direction.*—In determining the direction of the wind, it is to be observed that the *true*, not the magnetic, direction is to be recorded, and care must be taken in beginning observations that the cardinal points are accurately determined once for all. When the observations are made from a vane, this should be perfectly clear of trees, buildings, or anything likely to deflect the course of the wind, and the vane must have constant attention in case of working stiffly or " sticking," especially during frost. When possible it is better on the whole to make the observations directly from a flat roof or similar exposed situation. Draw a " compass-card," twelve or fourteen feet in diameter, on the ground or roof, and standing in the centre, turn so as to face the wind ; then read off the direction from the " compass-card."

Anyone possessing a little mechanical skill can easily construct a self-recording wind-vane for himself. A small vane is attached to a suitable spindle—an old " jenny " spindle will answer the purpose—which revolves in bushes fixed in the ends of a long narrow box, the end carrying the vane protruding. Inside the box the spindle carries a cylinder about four inches in diameter, and extending through nearly its whole length. An upright fixed beside the cylinder is grooved so as to allow a small pencil or siphon pen to work up and down, moved by a simple adaptation of the " works " of an American clock. A piece of smooth-surfaced paper is attached to the cylinder after the manner of a newspaper envelope, and revolves with changes of wind-direction, the spindle being moved by the vane. In contact with the paper the pen is drawn upwards by the clock at a given rate, and a record of every change is traced. The paper can be removed by slitting it longitudinally. The record will, in most cases, be found to be a band of varying width, according to the unsteadiness of the wind ; the average direction may be obtained by drawing a line down the centre of the band.

In making observations of wind direction it is well to record to the nearest point : and then in calculating the mean direction to halve all the " by " directions (N. by E., N.E. by N., etc.) between the two points on each side—counting half the N. by E.'s to N. and half to N.N.E., half the N.E. by N. to N.N.E. and half to N.E., and so on. This reduces to sixteen points, and the process may be repeated so as to reduce to eight points N., N.E., E., etc.

105. *Wind Pressure and Velocity: Anemometers.*—Many and various appliances have been devised for measuring the pressure and velocity of the wind, but none have as yet proved altogether satisfactory, either on account of defects in the instruments themselves, or of the difficulty of interpreting the records. Of velocity anemometers, that of Robinson is on the whole the most practically useful, being strong and durable in construction, and also independent of the direction of the wind. It consists of a vertical spindle, arranged so as to rotate with the least possible friction, which carries at its upper end four radial arms at right angles to each other, and at the extremity of each arm a hemispherical cup. The cups are arranged with their convex sides pointing in the same direction, and hence, whatever the direction of the wind, two opposite cups present opposite faces to it. But the pressure against the concave side of one cup is greater than against the convex side of the one opposite to it, hence the whole system rotates, and always in the same direction, the convex side of the cups advancing. A counter records the number of turns made by the spindle. Apart from the fact that this instrument does not work satisfactorily in light winds, and that the frictional resistance offered by the spindle varies considerably with the temperature and the condition of the weather, a good deal of doubt still exists

about the reduction of the data given by it. The ratio of the velocity of the wind to that of the cups varies with the size of the instrument, and it is therefore necessary to adopt certain standard dimensions ; those officially recognised in this country are—Radius of cups, 4·5 inches ; length of arms (centre of cup to centre of spindle), 24 inches. It was long supposed that the numerical value of the ratio for an anemometer of this size, and indeed for all sizes, amounted to 3·0, but recent investigations[1] have shown pretty conclusively that this value is considerably too great, 2·1 being much nearer the truth. It may be pointed out that the wind velocities published in most meteorological records are affected by the erroneous value of this factor, and must therefore be handled with caution in any inquiry involving their use.

In the course of the researches just referred to, Dines describes what promises to be the first really satisfactory pressure anemometer. The fact that wind blowing against the mouth of an open tube causes an increase of pressure within it was many years ago applied by Lind to the measurement of wind pressure. In Lind's anemometer, which has undergone a number of modifications, the mouth of a tube is kept facing the wind by a vane, and the increase of pressure in it measured by a column of water in a siphon. But the indications of such an instrument are unsatisfactory on account of the changes of pressure at the other end of the tube. The quantity to be measured is the difference of pressure between the end exposed to the wind and the other, which cannot be maintained at an exactly constant amount. Dines solves the difficulty by exposing the other end also to the wind, but in such a manner that the pressure is reduced instead of increased—thereby not only rendering the instrument independent of accidental changes of pressure not due to the wind, but increasing the differences

[1] See Dines : *Quart. Jour. Met. Soc.,* vol. xviii., p. 132.

caused by it, and making them easier to measure accurately.[1]

From experiments with the tube and other anemometers, Dines gives the following equation connecting P, the wind pressure in lbs. per square foot, with V, its velocity in miles per hour.

$$P = \cdot 003 \ V^2.$$

106. *Estimation of Wind Force.*—From what has been said it will be apparent that exact instrumental measurements of air movements are not easily obtained, and in practice they are usually dispensed with, and a system of estimation based on the effects produced by winds of different strengths is substituted. It would appear at first sight that this method is extremely crude, and likely to give widely discordant results with different observers ; but experience has shown that a much better agreement is obtained than we might expect, closer indeed than is shown by most instrumental methods.

The scale most commonly employed is that devised by Sir F. Beaufort in 1806, usually called the "Beaufort scale." It ranges from 0 to 12, the former figure representing a calm, and the latter a hurricane of such violence as to reduce a ship to scudding under bare poles. The intermediate numbers were originally determined by the amount of sail a full-rigged ship would carry in a wind of the force to which they correspond, but it is scarcely necessary to detail them in that fashion here. A little practice will enable the observer to estimate the wind force simply by the "feel" of the wind as he faces it. The following hints may be useful :

Force 0 Calm.
    1 Light air.
    2 Very light breeze.
    3 Light breeze.

[1] For details see *Q. J. Met. Soc.*, xvi., p. 2c8, and xviii., p. 168.

4 Moderate breeze.
5 Fresh breeze.
6 " Half a gale."
7 Moderate gale.
8 Fresh gale.
9 Strong gale.
10 " Whole gale."
11 Violent storm.
12 Hurricane.

Various other scales, differing in the range of numbers employed, are in use, such as the English land scale 0-6, the American international scale 0-10, and others.

107. *Diurnal Variation of Wind.*—If we bear in mind the relations of the upper to the lower currents explained in a former chapter we shall have no difficulty in understanding the diurnal variations in the direction and force of the wind, first fully accounted for by Sprung.[1] The upper current moves faster than the lower, and in the northern hemisphere follows a direction more to the *right*—in the southern more to the *left*. Now during the day the heating of the lower strata causes them to ascend, thereby increasing the friction between upper and lower currents, and reducing the difference of velocity. The lower current, under the influence of the upper, is deflected to the *right* in the northern hemisphere, to the *left* in the southern, and has its speed increased in both cases, while the upper, under the influence of the lower, is deflected in the opposite direction, and has its speed diminished ; and this effect is the more marked the greater the diurnal heating of the lower strata relatively to the upper, and the greater the normal angle between the two currents caused by friction of the lower on the earth's surface. Hence—

(1). Near the equator, and over the open sea, there is little diurnal variation either of direction or speed.

[1] *Met. Zeit.*, 1884, p. 16. *Lehrbuch der Meteorologie*, p. 342.

(2). On plains and similar land surfaces, even at great elevations, the wind shifts with the hands of a watch and attains its maximum strength during the afternoon, backing and diminishing again at night in the northern hemisphere. The changes of direction are reversed in the southern hemisphere.

(3). On mountain peaks the wind shifts *against* the hands of a watch, and diminishes in strength during the afternoon, and veers and increases again at night. The changes of direction are reversed in the southern hemisphere.

108. *Hygrometry.*—We have already hinted at two methods of determining the amount of aqueous vapour in the atmosphere ; one by actually abstracting the moisture in the form of water and weighing it, and another by cooling a bright surface till the temperature of the dew-point is indicated by the deposition of moisture. The first of these may be dismissed as useless for regular observations, and the second as requiring more time and manipulative skill than most observers have at their disposal. It accordingly becomes necessary to fall back on indirect methods, and of these we need only describe the one in almost universal use.

The psychrometer, the invention of which is variously ascribed to Hutton, Leslie, Gay-Lussac, and August, enables us to calculate the dew-point from the temperature of the air and the "temperature of evaporation." Two thermometers of exactly similar construction are placed side by side in the Stevenson screen. One of these is the common thermometer already described, and the bulb of the other is enveloped in a covering of thin muslin (perfectly clean and free from starch) kept wetted by a piece of cotton wick attached to it, which dips into a vessel of water.

As long as the air is dry, water evaporates from the wet muslin covering, and the heat required for the evaporation is drawn from the bulb of the thermometer, which accord ingly has its temperature lowered to what is called the "temperature of evaporation." A steady condition is reached, and from the difference between the readings of the dry and wet bulbs we find the dew-point.

The problem of calculating the dew-point from the temperatures of the air and of evaporation has been attacked by Ivory, August, Belli, Apjohn, Regnault, Kämtz, Clerk-Maxwell, Sworykin, Pernter, Ferrel, and Everett, from theoretical considerations, but none of the solutions hitherto offered are completely satisfactory. There seems to be little doubt that the equation required is of the form

$$f' - f'' = (t - t') \; K \; \frac{p}{P}$$

where f' = pressure of vapour at temperature of wet-bulb.

     f'' =   ,,   ,,   ,,   dew-point.

     t = temperature of dry bulb.

     t' =   ,,   wet bulb.

     p = barometric pressure at time and place of observation.

     P = a standard barometric pressure.

But K involves serious difficulties. For values of (t−t') such as are usually found in insular climates, it is best to use the empirical tables of Glaisher,[1] provided $\frac{p}{P}$ is nearly equal to unity. These tables cannot, however, be trusted for very low humidities, and are not applicable to observations made at high level stations.

109. *Absolute Humidity.*—The pressure of vapour actually existing in the atmosphere at any time, is, of course, the saturation pressure corresponding to the temperature of the dew-point, and is commonly known as the absolute humidity. The pressure indicated by the barometer is that due to the air and vapour together, but it must be observed that it is not the simple *sum* of the two pressures unless we assume that the air and vapour are completely mixed throughout, a

---

[1] 6th edition, 1876.

condition seldom if ever realised.[1]   Absolute humidity
shows two distinct types of diurnal variation.   Over the
ocean the curve has a single maximum and single minimum,
closely coinciding with those of temperature, and this simple
form occurs with little modification in damp climates or
during rainy periods generally.   In continental climates a
double maximum is found, one in the forenoon and another
in the late afternoon.   The minimum between is probably
caused by the supply of fresh vapour from the ground being
insufficient to replace that removed by the strong ascending
currents set up by the diurnal rise of temperature.

110. *Relative Humidity.*—Of greater practical importance
is the relative humidity, or ratio of the absolute humidity
to saturation.   It is usual to express this numerically as a percentage, saturation being represented by 100, *i.e.* by dividing
the vapour pressure corresponding to the dew-point by that
corresponding to the temperature of the air, and multiplying
by 100.   Since the diurnal variation of absolute humidity is
small in amount, the curve of relative humidity is practically
the inverse of that of temperature, and accordingly retains
almost the same form at all times and in all climates.

111. *Clouds: Classification of Different Kinds.*—The
condensation of vapour into visible form takes place in such
a manner as to give rise to an almost infinite variety of
cloud-shapes, and the classification of the different kinds of
clouds is a matter of great difficulty.   We may take it that
there are two distinct ways in which condensation most
frequently occurs—either a layer of the atmosphere is cooled
bodily to near its dew-point, or a body of moist air is in-
truded into a mass which is cold and dry.   The first may
happen through cooling by radiation, as in the case of air
lying in a valley during the night, or at an interface between
upper and under currents; and the result is a stratified

[1] See Strachey, *Proc. R. S.*, vol. xi., p. 182.

sheet of greater or less extent, forming a cloud which receives the generic title of *stratus*. The second, again, is usually the result of an ascending current caused by heating of the lower strata, in which the temperature falls till the dew-point is reached. As the ascending motion becomes weaker and weaker the air spreads out on all sides like the head of a sheaf, and the cloud takes a heaped or *cumulus* form.

Endless combinations of both stratus and cumulus forms are found at all levels, but beyond a certain elevation, probably that where the cloud-particles are frozen, special characteristics are observed, the structure of the cloud-masses taking a finer texture usually compared to hair or wool. All forms of this type are designated *cirrus*.

It is obvious that we may subdivide each of these great classes to any extent, so as to obtain any required degree of minuteness in description ; but however useful an elaborate classification may be to specialists, it is necessary for ordinary observing purposes to limit the number of terms employed.

Howard, in 1803, proposed the following cloud-nomenclature, which is still in general use[1] :—

1. CIRRUS. Parallel, flexuous, or diverging fibres, extensible by increase in any or all directions (" mares' tails ").
2. CUMULUS. Convex or conical heaps, increasing upward from a horizontal base.
3. STRATUS. A widely extended, continuous, horizontal sheet, increasing from below upward.
4. CIRRO-CUMULUS. Small well-defined roundish masses, in close horizontal arrangement or contact (the familiar " mackerel sky ").
5. CIRRO-STRATUS. Horizontal or slightly inclined masses attenuated towards a part or the whole of their cir-

[1] Essay on the Modifications of Clouds. *Phil. Mag.*, vol. vii.

cumference, bent downward, or undulated ; separate, or in groups consisting of small clouds having these characters.

6. CUMULO-STRATUS. The cirro-stratus blended with the cumulus, and either appearing intermixed with the heaps of the latter, *or superadding a widespread structure to its base.*

7. CUMULO-CIRRO-STRATUS OR NIMBUS. The rain cloud. A cloud, or system of clouds, from which rain is falling.

This classification is undoubtedly meagre, and although none of the efforts to improve upon it have proved entirely satisfactory, the following, proposed by Abercromby and Hildebrandsson [1] in 1887, was recommended for general use by the International Meteorological Conference at Munich in 1892.

High Clouds.

1. CIRRUS. Curl cloud. Average height 9,000 metres.
2. CIRRO-STRATUS. Average height 9,000 metres.
3. CIRRO-CUMULUS. Average height 6,500 metres.

Middle Clouds.

4. STRATO-CIRRUS. Average height ? metres.
5. CUMULO-CIRRUS. Average height 4,000 metres.

Low Clouds.

6. STRATO-CUMULUS. Average height 2,000 metres.
7. CUMULUS. Average top 2,000 ; base 1,500 metres.
8. CUMULO-NIMBUS OR CUMULO-STRATUS. Average top 3,000; base 1,500 metres.
9. NIMBUS. Average height 1,500 metres.
10. STRATUS. Average height 600 metres.

The numbers give the approximate average height at which each form of cloud is observed, based on the measure-

[1] *Q. J. Met. Soc.*, vol. xiii., No. 62, 1887.

ments of Ekholm and Hägstrom made at Upsala, and in the mountains of Jemtland. The observations of Clayton and Ferguson at Blue Hill Observatory, Massachusetts, give on the whole substantially the same figures for eastern America. The classification is similar to that of Howard, extended so as to distinguish an intermediate layer of clouds, Nos. 4 and 5. It would serve no good purpose to describe each in detail; the student is referred to Abercromby's photographs in the paper already quoted.[1]

A general classification of clouds becomes possible only in view of the fact established by Abercromby, that cloud-forms are identical in all parts of the world, which simply means that the processes of condensation take place everywhere in the same way. This, however, does *not* mean that the same cloud-forms are everywhere associated with the same kind of weather.

112. *Amount of Cloud.*—The amount of cloud is usually registered by considering that part of the sky more than 20° above the horizon, and estimating the fraction obscured to the nearest tenth; thus overcast sky is recorded as ten, half covered as five, and so on. Recent investigations at Pavlovsk[2] have shown that the error of this method may amount to 10 per cent., even with careful observation, and it seems desirable that greater accuracy should be obtained. The proportion of sky covered does not vary greatly at different hours of the day, but there is, in general, a tendency towards a maximum of stratiform clouds near the hour of minimum temperature, and of cumulus clouds towards the afternoon; the actual resulting variation depending, of course, on the local conditions favouring the formation of each kind. The observations of H.M.S. *Challenger*[3] show

---

[1] See also *Nature*, vol. 37, p. 129. *Cloud Atlas*, by Neumayer, Köppen, and Hildebrandsson, Hamburg, 1890; also K. Singer, *Cloud-forms*, Ackermann, Munich, 1892.

[2] *Repertorium für Meteorologie*, Bd. xiii.

[3] *Challenger Reports*, " Atmospheric Circulation," p. 28.

a double maximum—at, or shortly after, sunrise, and early in the afternoon ; and Liznar[1] gives the following four types of curve at different places :—

Madrid.—One maximum at noon, minimum in evening.

Los Angeles.—One morning maximum, minimum at noon.

Vienna.—Two maxima and minima ; principal maximum morning, principal minimum evening.

Tiflis.—Two maxima and minima ; principal maximum noon, principal minimum evening.

113. *Height of Clouds.*—According to Ekholm and Hügstrom, the height at which all forms of clouds occur increases from morning to night, except the summits of cumulus clouds, which are highest about 1·30 p.m. The observations of Clayton, at Blue Hill, indicate that the base of cumulus is also highest in the early afternoon, although both observers agree that the vertical thickness is greatest at that time. The daily change of level is less the greater the elevation.

114. *Precipitation.*—Under the term precipitation is included the total aqueous deposit on the earth's surface from the atmosphere, whether as rain or in the various wholly or partially frozen forms of snow, hail, or sleet. The physical processes involved in the formation of the different kinds of deposition are by no means well understood, and it is usual in making measurements to class all together as " rainfall " ; snow, hail, etc., being melted into water and measured as such.

The amount of rain falling on the earth's surface at any place is measured in terms of the depth to which that surface would be covered supposing none of the rain to be absorbed, and the object of the rain gauge is to expose a certain limited area so that it shall receive the same amount of rain as the surface of the ground in its immediate neighbourhood, no more and no less, and retain all the water so received for measurement. The depth of water collected over that

Met. Zeit., 1885, p. 342.

area represents the rainfall, and accuracy of measurement is attained by transferring the water to a narrow vessel. If, for example, the area of the rain gauge is twenty square inches, and the rainfall ·05 of an inch, we avoid the necessity of measuring this inconveniently small quantity by pouring the water into a measuring glass two square inches in section, which will be filled to a depth of half an inch, a length easily measured to the required degree of accuracy by means of a scale engraved on the side of the vessel.

The most convenient rain gauge for practical purposes consists of a copper or japanned tin cylinder, at the upper end of which is fixed a *turned* brass ring with a sharp edge whose diameter is accurately known. Some six inches below the ring the cylinder narrows to a funnel, and a tube leads to a collecting vessel (Fig. 23). The ratio of the area of the brass ring to the sectional area of the measuring glass must, of course, be accurately known. Wild has shown that the size of the gauge does not appreciably affect the results, at least within the limits of four and twenty-four inches diameter. The sizes usually employed in this country are five and eight inches.

The rain gauge should be exposed on a level piece of ground, clear of all objects whose height is greater than their distance from the gauge. The rim of the gauge, which must be perfectly level, is usually placed at a height of one foot above the ground, an adjustment of great importance, as the rainfall diminishes rapidly as the height above ground increases, at least until sixty feet is reached.

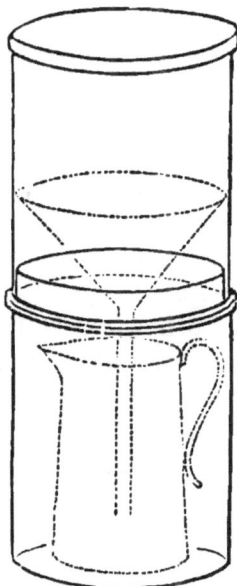

Fig. 23.

In describing the climate of any locality, it is important to know not only the total amount of rain, but the rate at which it fell. Two stations may have almost the same annual rainfall, but while one receives the bulk of it in a few weeks of torrential rains, the other has it spread over months of misty drizzle. For the accurate determination of the rate of fall it would be necessary to employ a continuously self-recording gauge, but for most purposes it is sufficient merely to record the number of "rainy days." Meteorologists are unfortunately not unanimous in defining a rainy day. Symons, to whom the rainfall organisation in Britain in great part owes its existence, adopts a minimum record of 0·01 inch as characteristic of a rainy day; Hann[1] suggests 1 mm. (·04 in.). The matter is simply a question of how much is to be allowed for accidental deposits, as dew or hoar-frost, and for errors of observation.

Of all meteorological phenomena, rainfall is the most variable and uncertain. In determining the average fall at any place, it is necessary to deal with observations extending over a long period, and hence in any general discussion great caution must be exercised. Until within the last few years, the number of stations furnishing rainfall observations oftener than once a day was extremely small, and it is impossible to speak in general terms as to the hourly variation. According to Hellman,[2] the diurnal variation of rainfall, like that of cloudiness, can be classified according to a number of typical curves. An afternoon maximum occurs in many places, especially in summer, corresponding to the hour of maximum frequency of thunderstorms; and another maximum late at night or in the very early hours of the morning is connected with peculiarities in the diurnal march of pressure, temperature, and wind-velocity. The latter phase is characteristic of Western Europe at all seasons, and

[1] *Met. Zeit.*, 1888, p. 39.
[2] *Met. Zeit.*, 1889, p. 271.

is always specially strong in winter. Symons[1] gives as tentative results from twenty years' observations in London— (1) In winter the nights are wetter than the days. (2) In spring and autumn there is not much difference. (3) In summer nearly half as much again falls by day as by night.

115. *Evaporation.*—The amount of water returned to the atmosphere by evaporation from the earth's surface is an element of the greatest importance in meteorological investigations, especially in its bearings on agricultural problems. Its measurement is, however, a matter of very great difficulty, and no simple instrument has as yet given sufficiently good results to justify its coming into general use.

[1] *British Rainfall,* 1885, p. 25.

CHAPTER VII.

THE ELEMENTS OF CLIMATE.

116. *Method of Inquiry.*—In order to gain an adequate conception of the climate of any part of the earth's surface, it is necessary in the first place to know what types of weather most frequently occur at different seasons, their average intensity and persistency, and the probable deviations at any given time from the usual state of things. We have already learned something of the conditions, so far as they are known, which favour the formation of one or other of these types, and it remains now to consider more particularly what are the general effects produced. Given the average type of weather, what are the principal modifications to which it is subject?

Now, in answering this question, the method to be followed is still the same. In dealing with weather, we treated it as the variable quantity, regarding everything else as constant. We now propose to regard the weather as a constant or a known variable, and to inquire what other factors go to make up climate, whether they are variable or not, and within what limits. But since in most cases the vicissitudes and variations of weather extend through a wide range, we shall not be justified in regarding any of its elements as constant except by employing carefully determined averages covering a very large number of cases. So great are these variations that we were able to describe, and in part to account for many of the phenomena observed without the presence of other variables (tacitly assumed, for the

136

time, to be constant), being even suggested ; and as soon
as other variables were looked for, it became necessary to
employ more refined methods of observation in order to de-
tect them.

This much was gathered originally from one exception,
which, as it were, proved the rule.   In lower latitudes,
where the sun's heat is of great intensity, the phenomena of
diurnal variation attain so full a development that instead of
being completely disguised by the weather disturbances, as
in higher latitudes, the case is frequently reversed.   The
diurnal variations in temperate zones, although not in general
so well-marked either absolutely or in relation to the weather
disturbances, are nevertheless important elements of climate.
We have already had occasion to discuss them as fully as
limits of space permit while describing the methods and
instruments employed in their measurement.   In still higher
latitudes, as the sun's power diminishes, the diurnal march
of phenomena becomes smaller and smaller in extent, until
a point is reached beyond which at certain seasons day and
night do not occur, and any small horary variation, if observed, must be due to the indirect influence of other parts
of the atmosphere.

Hence the inquiry is still further reduced to the question
—If over a certain area the average weather and the average
daily variations are the same, is the climate uniformly the
same at all points ?

117. *Land and Sea.*—We have hitherto divided the surface of the earth into land and water simply with reference
to the broad distinctions between the two in respect of
thermal properties ; we have regarded the sea as a fixed
surface having certain peculiarities of behaviour as to
radiation, absorption, reflection, etc., and the land as a
similar and similarly-situated surface having certain others.
This division may suffice as long as we are dealing with
general weather systems affecting large areas, but it obviously leaves many considerations out of account which,

reacting on these systems, must seriously modify the effects produced by them in different places.

Let us examine, then, the effects produced by winds blowing across different kinds of surfaces, and how these effects react upon the atmosphere. In discussing the incurving of wind in cyclones we compared the friction of air moving over the sea and of that moving over land, and we saw how the effects of such friction became less marked at small elevations, disappearing gradually, and showing quite clearly the friction between one layer of air and those immediately above and below it ; or in other words, the *viscosity* of the air. All the friction effects observed in the atmosphere are probably due to viscosity. There is always a very thin layer of air touching the earth's surface over which the others slide, and this contact layer is practically fixed to the surface, so that there is no slipping friction properly so called. The next layer drags over the fixed one, and again the next over that, and so on.

The effects of this process on a land surface are obvious enough. Over a plain country there will be a uniform dragging, which, over a broken or mountainous surface, will show an irregular increase, and extend on the whole to considerably higher levels.

118. *Oceanic Climates.*—But over the sea the case is markedly different. The dragging force on the surface produces a movement of the water corresponding to its amount and persistency, and ultimately gives rise to a surface current ; and since the water has more inertia and greater specific heat than the air, the current penetrates further than the wind which causes it, and acts as a kind of brake on the fluctuations of temperature of the winds passing over it. Hence where the prevailing winds blow landwards from the sea they bring with them the climate of the region whence they came, retaining the oceanic temperature characteristics of small range and deferred maxima and minima. Again, when the prevailing winds are seawards

from the land, the surface water is driven away from the coast, and bottom water, varying little in temperature, comes welling up from below.[1]

It is matter of observation that these two causes acting together supplement the transference of heat brought about by the winds. Warm water is carried from lower latitudes to higher, and cold from higher to lower, with the result that on the whole in the tropical zones the continents are warmer than the oceans, while the reverse is the case in higher latitudes.

Since the annual range of air temperature over the sea is much less than over the land, it follows that, if the mean of the former for the whole year is the higher, the greatest differences must occur in winter. In the temperate zones the excess of cold over continental, compared with oceanic areas, in winter, is greater than the excess of heat in summer. The following average temperature for each month at Valentia in the extreme west of Ireland, and at Voronezh in Central Russia, in almost the same latitude, may be taken as an example :—

	Valentia. Lat. 51°·55′ N.	Voronezh. Lat. 51° 44′ N.	Diff.
January, . .	45°·3 F.	16°·4 F.	+ 28°·9
February, . .	45·5	16·7	+ 28·8
March, . .	46·3	36·9	+ 19·4
April, . . .	49·0	44·4	+ 4·6
May, . . .	52·8	60·4	− 7·6
June, . . .	56·3	68·3	− 12·0
July, . . .	58·7	70·6	− 12·2
August, . . .	59·5	67·9	− 8·4
September, . .	56·6	57·1	− 0·5
October, . .	52·0	44·3	+ 7·7
November, . .	47·6	34·1	+ 13·5
December, . .	45·4	22·5	+ 22·9
Year, . . .	51·3	44·2	+ 7·1

[1] *Scottish Geographical Magazine*, 1888, p. 345.

119. *The Atlantic Ocean.*—The best illustration of these facts is afforded by the ocean most familiar to us—the North Atlantic. The prevailing winds are there determined, as already stated, by the "Atlantic anti-cyclone," and by an area of low pressure whose centre remains stationary in the neighbourhood of Iceland : and of these the former attains its fullest development in summer, and the latter in winter.

Fig. 24. *February.*   Fig. 25. *August.*

NORTH ATLANTIC OCEAN.

Sea 0° to 5° F. warmer than Air. ||| 5° to 10° F. ||| 10° to 15° F. ||| Air 0° to 5° F. warmer than Sea. ///

Hence the North Atlantic forms an immense anti-cyclonic vortex, weakened and deformed in winter by the depression to the north, which receives cold north-westerly winds from the great winter anti-cyclone over Canada, and gives south-westerly winds (the great cyclone track) to western Europe.

The chart recently published by H.S.H. the Prince of Monaco[1] shows that the surface currents in the North Atlantic

Comptes rendus, t. cxiv., 8th Feb., 1892.

are in great measure determined by these prevailing winds, the average velocity for the whole of the ocean amounting to $4\frac{1}{2}$ nautical miles in twenty-four hours, and the centre of rotation coinciding closely with that of the Atlantic anti-cyclone in the region of the Saragasso Sea.

The corresponding temperature effects are well shown in Figs. 24 and 25, which divide the North Atlantic into regions where the air is warmer or colder than the sea, or where both have the same temperature, during the two extreme months February and August. We observe, generally, that in accordance with the principles just explained—

(1) When wind and current move east or west, air and sea have the same temperature.
(2) When both move northwards, the air cools faster than the water, and the sea is warmer than the air.
(3) When both move southwards, the air heats faster than the water, and the sea is cooler than the air.

Fig. 26 shows how these conditions determine the annual range of air temperature, *i.e.* the difference between the hottest and coldest months (August and February). Between 45° and 55° N. lat. the prevailing westerly winds coming from the American continent are slowly cooled in summer and warmed in winter, the range

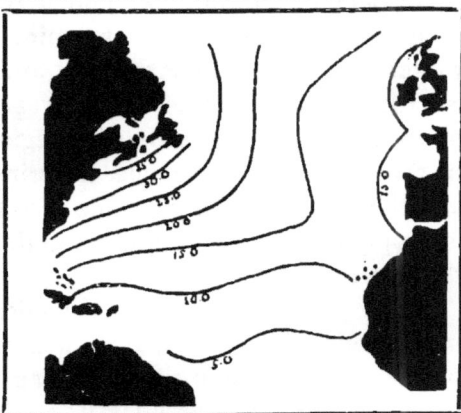

Fig. 26.

decreasing to 20° F. in 49° W. long., and to 15° in 30°

W. long. Still further east, where the winds are more southerly, the drift current from the Gulf Stream carries a line of minimum range close to the coast of Europe, the increase caused by the proximity of the Continent being scarcely felt 200 miles from land. The retardation in the annual charges of temperature, produced by the same cause as that which diminishes their amplitude, is well shown by the fact that, if we draw a line from Valentia through Mullaghmore to the Pentland Firth, thence to Heligoland, and through Danzig, Riga, and St. Petersburg to Archangel, almost all stations north and west of this line have the lowest monthly average of temperature in February, while all to south and east have it in January ; and in the former area the annual maximum is markedly later than in the latter.[1]

On the eastern seaboard of America the distribution is considerably complicated by the presence of the Arctic or Labrador current, which penetrates southward as far as Cape Hatteras between the Gulf Stream and the coast.

If we follow the meridian of 65° W. from the coast of Nova Scotia southward, we find a rapid decrease of annual range, chiefly due to the warming of the north-westerly winter winds of Arctic America ; and after the Gulf Stream is crossed the decrease becomes gradually slower. South of 30° N. lat., in the trade wind region on the southern side of the Atlantic anti-cyclone, the winds are always easterly, and the currents take the same direction ; the smaller range is simply caused by the greater uniformity of the seasons in the lower latitudes.

Along with these chiefly mechanical effects we must take into account the evaporation which goes on from the surface of the sea. Oceanic winds, having an unlimited supply of moisture, are never very far from the point of saturation ;

---

[1] See also G. Schwalbe : *Ueber die Maxima und Minima der Temperatur.* Berlin, 1892.

according to the *Challenger* observations the average relative humidity in the North Atlantic is about 80 per cent. Hence a very slight reduction of temperature, whether by radiation or by contact with a cold body, produces fog or mist. Condensation of this kind occurs most frequently where a warm air-current meets a colder, or passes over a region where the surface of the sea is abnormally cold, or again where it comes in contact with a cold land surface. We shall have occasion later to discuss the last case in detail; for the others we need only mention such examples as the great fog-banks of Newfoundland, the Norwegian coast, and the coast of Peru.

The effect of strong evaporation upon the sea itself, in relation to its influence on currents through increase of the density of the water, belongs more properly to the province of oceanography than of meteorology.

120. *Continental Climates.*—The source of the great differences between oceanic and continental climates lies of course in the much greater variations of temperature to which the air over a land area is exposed. But it must be borne in mind that these excessive fluctuations are limited to the surface of the earth and to the strata of air lying immediately upon it. If we ascend an isolated peak, which enables us to gain a considerable elevation, but does not present sufficient horizontal surface to materially disturb the temperature gradients as does a high plateau or range of mountains, we find a gradual decrease in the variations of temperature, and a transition to the climatic conditions found over the ocean. For example, at the low level observatory of the Puy de Dôme, situated in a valley where radiation effects are strongly marked, the mean annual range of temperature is 32°·4 F., while at the peak, 3,500 feet higher, it amounts to only 24°·3 F.[1]

Since, then, we are dealing only with a thin layer next

[1] Woeikof, *Met. Zeit.*, 1892, p. 373.

the surface, it is evident that so long as the surface is level there will be little tendency towards horizontal motion ; all the temperature changes at the surface will simply go to produce more or less local convection currents like the familiar whirls on a dusty road on a calm hot summer day. When the heating and cooling is unequal, pressure will be on the whole less over the warmer than the colder areas, and a movement of air will begin from the latter towards the former. Along a coast line we find the diurnal phenomenon of land and sea breezes : during the day the land is hotter than the sea ; the air over it rises, and its place is taken by air brought in by the sea breeze : again, during the night the land is colder than the sea ; the air over it sinks and flows towards the lower pressure as the land breeze. Similarly, a land area, liable to be greatly heated and cooled by radiation, shows the seasonal alternations analogous to land and sea breezes, usually termed *monsoons ;* when the land is hotter than the sea surrounding it, a constant wind blows in towards it, and when colder, away from it.

121. *Effect of Mountains.*—As we have said, little intensity can be developed in either of these cases as long as the land surface is level. In the northern parts of Central Africa, where the power of the sun's rays is enormous and some of the highest known temperatures have been recorded, there is little circulation of a definite character ; at such stations as Murzuk, Shimmedru, Ghadames, and Kuka almost every second day is calm, while at Cairo calms average one day in four. Although within the trade wind region, Alice Springs in the heart of Australia averages more than one calm day in three.

But if the land surface is elevated so as to form a cone, or high plateau with long sloping sides, the thin stratum lying next the surface will, when cooled, tend to flow downwards and outwards, and will flow faster the steeper the slope. Again, when this stratum is heated it will tend to rise. We

know that the temperature of the whole mass of the atmosphere decreases as we ascend.   But the heating effect of
the sun's rays on a land surface is nearly the same at all
elevations, hence the greater the elevation the greater the
difference of temperature between the layer of air next the
ground and the great body of the atmosphere at that elevation, and therefore the greater the tendency to ascend.   For
example, suppose the layer next the ground to be 100 feet
thick.   Let the normal temperature at sea level be 40° F.,
then, assuming an average vertical temperature gradient of .
1° F., in 300 ft. for the whole of the lower atmosphere, the
normal temperature at a height of 3,000 feet will be 30° F.
If now the 100 feet layer be heated to 60° F. throughout, at
sea level it will be 20° F. warmer than the surrounding air,
but at a height of 3,000 feet on a mountain slope the difference will be 30° F., and therefore the ascending tendency
correspondingly greater.

Ferrel[1] aptly compares the case of warm and rarefied air
ascending a slope to that of warm air rising in a flue.   If
the flue is horizontal there is little circulation, no matter how
hot the air in it compared with that outside ; but even a slight
inclination sets up a strong current, and the current is
stronger the greater the difference of temperature inside and
outside, as we know from the fact that the draught in a
chimney is best in cold weather.   With the same temperature inside the flue, *i.e.* in the stratum of air next the
ground, we obtain the "cold weather" conditions at high
levels.

Hence, we find invariably that land and sea breezes
and monsoon winds never attain a marked development unless there are mountains or high lands in the immediate
neighbourhood.   The strongest land and sea breezes known
are experienced at Port Royal in Jamaica, in the vicinity of
the Blue Mountains ; and, notwithstanding the compara-

[1] *Popular Treatise on the Winds*, p. 197.

K

tively weak insolation and the many disturbing causes, the high lands of Dartmoor produce marked land and sea breezes at Plymouth during favourable anti-cyclonic conditions. The north-east or winter monsoon of the Indian Ocean, although really superposed on the trade winds, never rises above a moderate breeze, while the south-west monsoon, drawn towards the Himalayas, is usually almost a gale.

122. *Mountains and High Land as Obstacles to Air Currents.*—Assuming the existence of a wind blowing from the sea to the land, we come to the effect produced on the air current by meeting an obstacle, such as a range of hills. Looking first at the purely mechanical problem, let us suppose that the wind advances exactly at right angles to the coast-line, and meets a straight line of cliffs, from the summit of which a table-land extends for some distance inland. Here we have a case analogous to that of water rushing out of a dock over the "sill." The main stream, on meeting the sill, jumps clear of it, and travels for some distance before losing its upward deflection. Fig. 27 represents a vertical section through the stream. On the face of the sill at A, pressure is

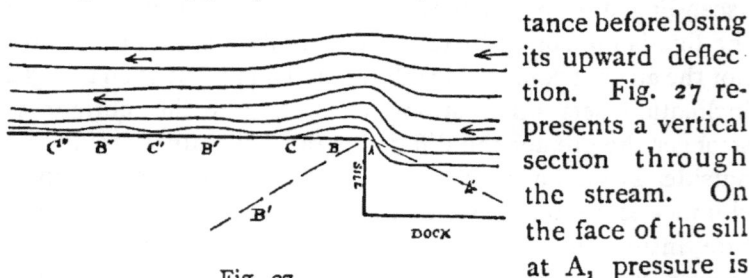

Fig. 27.

increased and the motion diminished, and above, at B, pressure is diminished and the rate of motion increased. At C matters begin to assume their normal course. The space B forms a kind of slack water in which rotary or vortex motion is set up, the vortices gradually "tailing off" towards C. After passing C a certain amount of undulatory motion is retained for a time, and waves C B' C', C' B" C", etc., similar to A B C, succeed each other, rapidly diminishing in size.

Suppose, now, that the wall of the dock, instead of being vertical as at A, slopes, as shown by the dotted line A'. The upward deflection will then evidently be diminished, and the undulations will be smaller the more A' is inclined. Again, if the sill, instead of being horizontal, slopes downwards as at B', the undulating motion will be greatly increased, and the slack water space at B, with its rotating vortices, correspondingly enlarged. These conditions represent the case of wind passing over an irregular undulating country, or over the crest of a range of mountains. Every inequality on the earth's surface deflects the air upwards from its weather side, and forms a region of confused irregular whirls on the lee side. Whence we may form some idea of the enormous difficulties in the way of studying the general motions of the atmospheric ocean where our observations are largely restricted to the eddying movements round pebbles at the bottom.

The justness of the analogy between the motions of air and water must be established by observations of the former. These have been made by Cleveland Abbe [1] and others with the help of kites, and much may be learned by observing the frequent smoke vortices on the lee side of a tall chimney. But the most abundant data are afforded by the winds themselves.

123. *Effect of Mountains on Rainfall.*—When a current laden with moisture from the sea is forced upwards by an obstacle in its path its temperature is at once reduced and the aqueous vapour it contains condensed, first into cloud, then into rain. Hence, universally, the regions of greatest rainfall are found where a prevailing wind from the sea meets high land at a short distance from the coast. The British Islands, where with prevailing winds from the Atlantic and a watershed running nearly north and south, the annual

[1] See his elementary discussion of this subject. *Repor. of Chief Signal Officer*, 1889, Appendix 15.

rainfall on the western side averages nearly one half more than that on the eastern, are a familiar example. Still more striking are the effects of the Western Ghâts and the Khasia mountains on the south-west monsoon. The mountains being excessively steep, the monsoon current has to rise through a great height while crossing only a small tract of country, and we accordingly find such phenomenal falls as 250 inches at Mahableshwar, and 474 inches at Chirra Punji. We have here obviously another force strengthening the ascending currents in mountainous regions. The latent heat set free by condensation goes to raise the temperature of the air, and therefore to increase the tendency to ascend.

After the obstacle is surmounted the air, largely deprived of its moisture and no longer forced to ascend, becomes dry, and it is not, in general, possible to follow its motion by means of cloud. The region of vortex motion corresponding to B (Fig. 27) can, however, frequently be recognised ; for, since pressure is there somewhat reduced, the air coming over the summit is drawn in, and being cooled by expansion again becomes saturated, and a thin wreath of cloud is formed which presents the appearance of a "smoking mountain."

124. *Helm and Helm Bar.*—When, after crossing a mountain ridge, the current begins to descend on the other side, it is sometimes unable to dislodge the mass of air lying below, which then acts like the dock sill and continues the undulating motion. The current reflected upward is thus again cooled, sometimes until another cloud is formed. Hence the phenomena of the " helm and helm bar " seen on Cross Fell and the Eden Valley, and the " Table Cloth " and bar of Table Mountain.[1] The application of this principle may be further extended by supposing the obstacle analogous to the dock sill to be wholly air, and we are

[1] See *Quart. Jour. Met. Soc.,* xv., p. 103.

brought back to the frictional effects of an upper current moving upon an under, and the formation of waves and ripples on the surface of the latter as shown by "mackerel skies," "Noah's Arks," and other forms of cirro-cumulus cloud.

125. *Obstacles not at Right Angles to Currents.*—For the sake of clearness we have restricted ourselves to the case of currents meeting an obstacle exactly at right angles. In the general case where the obstacle is more or less inclined, part of the current is forced upwards, and part deflected so as to flow along the side of the obstacle, the relative proportions of the two parts depending on the angle of inclination; just as in a stream dammed by a weir part of the water flows over the weir and part is deflected into the mill-race. The rainfall of India during the south-west monsoon affords an excellent opportunity of studying such effects, little or no rain falling in regions where the current runs parallel to the mountains at a time when excessive amounts are recorded where the mountains are at right angles to it.[1]

We conclude then, generally, that the effect of high land or mountain ranges, towards which winds blow from the sea, is greatly to increase the cloudiness and rainfall on the weather side, and, as it were, discharge the oceanic qualities of the current so that on the lee side the climate becomes more that of a continent. The air, deprived of its moisture, sinks down under the shelter of the mountains, and especially in valleys remains comparatively undisturbed. This fact is at once apparent from the increase of solar and terrestrial radiation, as indicated by greater variations of temperature. In Fig. 28 lines are drawn through those parts of the British Isles having the same average annual range of temperature, and these show that, wherever the prevailing south-westerly winds meet elevated land, the range of tem-

[1] See *Scottish Geographical Mag.*, 1892, p. 248.

perature rapidly increases, and the maximum range invariably occurs in valleys and low country on the lee side, as
in Salisbury Plain, the Central and Eastern Plains, the
Plain of York, and Strathmore in Scotland. Again, where-
ever the belt of high land is interrupted the oceanic charac-

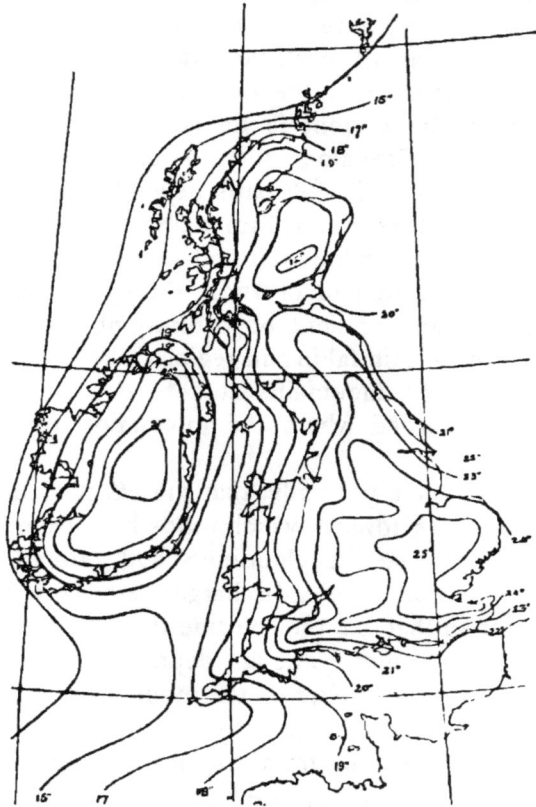

Fig. 28.

teristic of small range is retained much further eastward, as
in the Vale of Severn, the Cheshire Plain, the district between the Pennine Chain and the Cambrian Mountains,
and the Plain of Forth and Clyde.

126. *Variability of Temperature.*—Another method of discussing changes of temperature, introduced by Hann, shows the differences of climate in another way. If we calculate the mean difference of the temperature of each day from that of the next, we get the variability of the temperature, or probable change from day to day. Now, Hann's investigations show that the variability of temperature increases from the coast inland;[1] and, applying this to the British Isles, we find a variability of 1°·9 F. at Valentia and Falmouth, 2°·4 at Aberdeen, 2°·5 at Armagh, Glasgow, and Stonyhurst, 2°·7 at Kew, 3°·1 at Oxford, and 3°·4 at Makerstoun.[2] The two last named stations show a variability equal to that of such truly continental places as Cassel, Prague, or Budapest.

127. *Variations in the Nature of Surface: Snow-coverings.*—The distribution of land and sea, and the configuration of the land surfaces are, of course, constant quantities so far as our present purposes are concerned. We come next to variations due to different kinds of land surfaces. In a former chapter it was found that the conditions of temperature and moisture varied in different soils and exposures, and under different kinds of vegetation. These will be more conveniently discussed at a later stage, for they involve considerations outside the domain of meteorology proper.

The researches of Woeikof[3] and others have shown that apart from its effect on the soil the presence of a snow surface during a considerable part of the winter has a marked influence on climate. According to Zenker, a snow surface reflects about $\frac{1}{6}$ of the sun's rays falling upon it, while clear ground reflects only about $\frac{1}{30}$, hence snow is much less warmed during the day; and since during winter,

[1] *Met. Zeit.*, 1892., p. 46.
See R. H. Scott, *Proc. R. S.*, vol. xlvii., p. 303.
[3] See *Der Einfluss einer Schneedecke:* Geog. Abhandl., Wien, 1889.

under the anti-cyclonic conditions favourable to sunshine, the air is exceptionally dry and free from dust, little heat is absorbed by it. Again, from its feathery structure, dry snow contains large quantities of air, and it is therefore an extremely bad conductor of heat; and at the same time, from the nature of its surface, it radiates heat more freely at night than the surface of the ground. Thus with the same weather conditions the surface has a lower temperature when covered with snow, and the deficiency being communicated by conduction to the layer of air in contact with it, tends to increase the reversal of the vertical temperature gradient noticed in winter anti-cyclones (§ 71). The cold layer, on account of its weight, lies close to the snow surface, and as long as the snow remains, temperature seldom rises to the melting point even with strong sun. The rough surface of the snow offers considerable resistance to horizontal motion of air, and hence warm winds coming from other regions are weakened, and tend to rise above the cold surface layer. Snow is therefore favourable to the development and persistence of anti-cyclonic conditions, and a thaw is usually due to strong external influences, powerful enough to break up the anti-cyclone and dislodge the masses of cold air. In northern continental areas, such as Russia and Siberia, the extensive snow-sheets, lasting all through the winter, no doubt considerably increase the intensity of the anti-cyclones and the severity of the cold.

When the temperature of the air rises, the limitation imposed by the fact that the snow cannot become warmer than 32° F. makes itself felt. The warm air blowing from the open sea or from land free of snow, is cooled by contact with the snow, and still more by the abstraction of heat required for melting. Further, as the melting goes on the snow changes into ice; it no longer contains vast numbers of air spaces, and therefore becomes a better conductor of heat. Again, as the snow disappears, the ground is saturated with ice-cold water, and more heat is required to raise the temperature of the surface. Thus on the whole a thick snow-covering tends to intensify and continue the weather of winter, and to prevent the warmer weather of spring taking effect. An exceptionally cold winter is not so likely to be followed by a late spring as one in which the snowfall is unusually large.

128. *Recurrent Changes of Weather Type.*—Having sketched the main features of climate as determined by the distribution of land and sea, we may notice some results of the normal changes from one type of weather to another at different seasons of the year; reverting, in fact, to the consideration of weather as a variable. As our purpose is simply to illustrate a method, we confine ourselves to one or two examples.

129. *Interruptions of Temperature.*—By calculating the mean temperature of every day in the year at a number of representative stations in Scotland, Buchan[1] discovered the occurrence of certain interruptions in the annual march of temperature, which he arranges as follows :—

Six cold periods—

    1. 7th to 14th February.
    2. 11th to 14th April.
    3. 9th to 14th May.
    4. 29th June to 4th July.
    5. 6th to 11th August.
    6. 6th to 13th November.

Three warm periods—

    1. 12th to 15th July.
    2. 12th to 15th August.
    3. 3rd to 14th December.

[1] *Jour. Scot. Met. Soc.*, vol. ii., 1869, p. 4.

Some of these periods are familiar in weather lore. The second cold spell, which according to the old style occurs in the beginning of April, includes the " Borrowing Days."

> " March borrows frae April
> Three days, and they are ill.
> The first o' them is wun' and weet;
> The second it is snaw and sleet;
> The third of them is peel-a-bane,
> And freezes the wee bird's neb tae stane."

Similar sayings are found in many parts of Europe, notably in France and Andalusia. The third cold period is re-marked all over Europe, and is associated with the " ice saints," Mamertus, Pancratius, and Servatius, whose names the Bohemians run into Pan Serboni. They say " Pan Serboni withers the tree." So also in Russia " St. Isodor (14th May) is past; the north winds are over."

Buchan shows that all these interruptions depend on anomalies in the prevailing winds, fogs, or the rainfall, and they can be connected with a tendency to periodic changes in the type of weather recurring about the same time every year.

130. *Distribution of Rainfall.*—The changes of weather type are perhaps most marked in their effect upon the rain-fall. Since a change of type usually involves a redistribution of pressure and temperature over a very large area, it is easily understood that if the normal sequence is disturbed, such disturbance is likely to be persistent for a considerable time. If, for example, the Atlantic anti-cyclone does not extend as usual in early summer, it is probably prevented from doing so by a cause which will delay its extension for a considerable time, as happened in 1888, when easterly winds and cloudy skies prevailed almost throughout the summer. Hence, when a change of type brings with it a

periodic fall of rain, that fall is usually either up to time, or is considerably delayed.   This can be abundantly illustrated from folk-lore.

> " If St. Swithin weeps, the proverb says,
>   The weather will be foul for forty days,"

applies to the summer rains in the British Isles.   In other countries these rains are looked for at different dates, and we find the saint altered to suit; in the Haute Marne and Loire, *St. Medard* (June 8th); in the Province of Sarthe, *St. Calais* (June 1st) ; *Visitation of B. V. M.* (July 2nd), in Belgium and Austria ; *St. Anne* (July 26), in Northern Italy, and so on.

We remark again that the method involved here is simply that of probabilities ; and in making practical application of it the value of the probability must always be carefully determined.

CHAPTER VIII.

131. *Relation of Meteorology to other Sciences.*—The work of forecasting weather, and in particular of giving timely warning of destructive gales, is the first and most obvious practical application of meteorological science. From the sketch we have given of the general methods employed it appears that the problem is, in its larger aspects, wholly physical; ultimately a question of motion of a given fluid under given thermal conditions, and that the difficulties consist in completely defining the properties of the fluid and the conditions under which it moves.

But since no branch of science is independent of others, it is necessary for the specialist in one department to meet that in another half way, to arrange his data and results in a form which facilitates comparison. Specially is this the case with the group of subjects which has recently taken the family name of Physiography. Meteorology involves geography. Many geographical relations are dependent upon meteorology. Biology must take account of the conditions of life determined by climate, and these are the geology of the present. Narrowing the matter still further, the meteorologist finds three classes of practical questions with which he must deal : those of physical geography, or the influence of climate directly upon mountains and rivers, land and sea, etc. ; those of zoology, the distribution of animals, and, economically the most important, of food fishes ; and those of botany, the distribution of plants, agricultural products most important economically.

Of the first class it is unnecessary to speak further, inasmuch as meteorological results are so largely controlled and modified by geographical conditions that they are perforce expressed, as it were, in the first instance, in geographical terms, and the geographer finds his meteorological facts, so far as they are known, ready to his hand.

The relation of climate to the distribution of animals can as yet scarcely be said to admit of special discussion by the meteorologist except perhaps with regard to the human species. The range of any given species depends directly upon this element to only a very limited extent, according to its power of withstanding heat or cold, dampness or dryness, or of adapting itself to these varied conditions ; for intermediate factors come in, such as the distribution of animal food, of natural enemies and the like, which in turn depend both directly and indirectly upon climate. We should expect *à priori* that the fauna of any region would de-depend ultimately upon its climate, and of course we have rough classifications according to frigid, temperate, and torrid zones, but a closer relation remains to be traced. It may be said that in the case of food fishes a coincidence between particular weather conditions and the presence or absence of certain species has been clearly indicated, but the relation is not direct ; whether it depends upon surface forms upon which the fish feed or is connected with periodic reproductive changes is evidently not a meteorological question.

In the third case, that of plant life, the biological conditions are simpler, and the relations of climate at the same time more direct. For the individual plants cannot of themselves move from place to place, and the elements of climate are therefore so far constant and simpler than in the case of, for example, migrating animals. Again, plants derive their food partly from the air and partly from the soil, which is itself a chemical and mechanical product of meteorological action on known types of rock-formation.

There is thus a sufficiently definite problem stated, the final solution of which must of course rest with the botanist and agriculturist, but which requires the application of special methods to the meteorological data.

132. *Relations of Soil to Climate: Different kinds of Soils.* —The relations of soil to climate, in so far at least as the United States are concerned, have been discussed by Professor Hilgard[1] in a manner which affords excellent guidance to the agricultural meteorologist. Soil is defined as the residual product of the action of meteorological agencies upon rocks. First, mechanical agencies—(a) changes of temperature affecting the several constituent minerals of rocks differently, and thereby forming minute cracks which give access to water and air; (b) freezing water widening these cracks and breaking the rock up into fragments; (c) ice or glacier action, reducing rocks to fine powder, removing the material from the parent rock and depositing it as "till" or boulder clay; (d) flowing water, the most active agent at the present time, acting in a manner similar to glaciation but with less intensity and over a wider area so as to produce a deposit more variable in the size of its particles and more mixed in its ingredients. Second, chemical agencies—(a) solution by water alone, according to the solubility of the rock-forming minerals; (b) carbonic acid, always present in the air as the product of volcanic action, decay, fermentation, combustion, and the breathing of animals, being absorbed by rain water, greatly increases its solvent properties, decomposing the ingredients of the soil and rendering them available for plant nutrition; (c) oxygen, acting directly as well as in carbonic acid, chiefly in the formation of "rust" from the lower oxide of iron common in most green

[1] U.S. Department of Agriculture, Weather Bureau, Bulletin No. 3. 1892.

and black minerals; (*d*) water, entering directly into combination with substances present or newly formed in the
rocks, and thereby increasing their bulk and breaking up the
original structure; as in the formation of clay from felspars.

These forces produce different results according to the relative parts played by each, and to the nature of the material
upon which they act. Soils may be classified according to
position into residual or sedentary, which rest upon the rock
from which they have been formed by weathering, and
transported soils, which are either *colluvial*—moved a short
distance by water, gravity, or wind, without undergoing any
arrangement as to size of particles, or *alluvial*—deposited
regularly in beds or strata from flowing water. Or, they may
be regarded as consisting of rock, clay, and vegetable matter,
each in different proportions and in different stages of
powdering and decomposition; and as such described as
light or sandy, heavy or clayey, and humus.

133. *Action of Weather in Formation of Soils.*—The
climatic factors involved in the formation of soil are therefore chiefly the temperature and the amount and seasonal
distribution of the rainfall. According to Hilgard, temperature changes take effect through the greater chemical
activity at high temperatures and the more rapid breaking
up of material when the range of variation is large. Rainfall
acts for the most part by leaching or washing out the more
soluble ingredients from soils already formed by weathering,
to an extent depending on their permeability : light sandy
soils may be washed to a great depth, while heavy clays allow
the water to run directly off their surface. The formation
of clay itself is an important instance of this action. When
a granitic rock has been crumbled down by mechanical
agencies—variations of temperature, freezing of water in its
pores and so on—the rain water containing carbonic acid
removes the potash from the felspar and mica in the form
of carbonate of potash, while the silicate of alumina and the

quartz are separated by the action of the water; the former being much lighter than the latter, is washed away and re-deposited as *clay*. This process is obviously impossible where the rainfall is scanty, and loose sandy or dusty soils accordingly predominate in arid climates. Hence also the sharp distinction between surface and sub-soils, familiar in humid regions, does not occur in dry. Hilgard quotes an instance of tomatoes, water-melons, etc., growing better on soil freshly dug from a depth of 7 to 10 feet than on sur-face soil, in the dry climate of Nevada City, California.

The formation of humus or vegetable mould is also largely dependent upon climate. Vegetable matter exposed to the influence of hot rainless summers is "burnt up"—destroyed by a slow combustion which leaves little residue beyond the mineral ash. On the other hand, when saturated with or submerged in water it is transformed into a sub-stance of which the extreme form is peat—a sour soil, partly soluble, as we know from the bitter coffee-coloured water which drains from it. Such land must be reclaimed by drainage and the use of lime, which neutralizes its acidity and gradually changes the peaty matter into insoluble black humus. This last, the true black mould desired of the farmer, is formed by decomposition underground in pro-perly drained land, the essential conditions being a certain amount of moisture, sufficient to keep the decaying matter moist, but without stagnation to allow of its becoming acid or sour. Hence humus is much less plentiful in dry than in humid climates. In the arid districts of America strawy manure cannot be ploughed-in raw from the lack of moisture to cause fermentation. It is necessary either to "cure" the manure before laying it down, or to moisten by irrigation; otherwise it is simply reduced to ashes by slow combustion, a process which may occupy two or three years.

In like manner the soils of humid and arid regions may be contrasted with reference to other ingredients. Lime is in the former dissolved out in the form of carbonate and transferred from the surface into the sub-soil, and from uplands into lowlands and valleys ; while in the latter it remains more uniformly distributed. Poor land is for this reason less frequent in arid regions, which for the most part become, when irrigated, amazingly fertile. Again, in the process of clay-making, zeolites are usually formed ; and in these complex hydrous silicates, potash wherever present takes precedence of soda. Hence when a potash solution comes in contact with a zeolite containing soda, the soda is replaced by potash and washed away. Soils retain potash tenaciously, but soda only when the rainfall is insufficient to wash it out, as in the case of alkali lands.

Many of these results, derived by Hilgard from observations of natural processes on a large scale, are simply further confirmation of those arrived at by Sir J. B. Lawes and Dr. Gilbert at the experimental station at Rothamsted, from which we may extend our consideration of the same modes of action to their application to the behaviour of various manures, the development of roots, and so on. Thus with dry weather between autumn and spring the soil retains the nitrates left over from former dressings, which would otherwise be drained off ; a mild spring allows roots to penetrate to a great depth in search of food ; and favouring rains later in the season become concentrated solutions of plant food as they soak into the soil.

It is, therefore, abundantly evident that a close examination of the effects of climatic agencies on soil alone is of the first importance in agriculture. The points to be studied are (1) temperature of the soil in relation to the temperature of the air and to radiation—depending on (a) the nature and colour of the surface, (b) the exposure, (c) the conductivity of the soil, (d) drainage ; (2) moisture of the soil in relation to rainfall—depending on (a) its permeability

L

(*b*) retentive power. Much remains to be done in investigating some of the heads just enumerated, and considering the endless variety of conditions involved it must always be difficult to apply general rules to any particular case. We may, however, state the results arrived at in some instances. The temperature variations of the surface of the soil and their relations to the nature of that surface, and to the conductivity of the soil, have already been noticed (§ 33). When the rainfall is fairly distributed throughout the year, and the winter snow-covering interrupted and irregular, the mean temperature of the soil closely agrees with that of the air ; but where there are prolonged seasons of drought, or where the ground is long covered with snow, considerable differences may occur. The greater diathermancy of the air in the higher layers of the atmosphere causes a marked increase in the power of the sun's rays in mountainous regions, hence while the air is not heated to the same extent the soil becomes relatively much warmer, a fact of great importance in connection with the distribution of plants and animals ;[1] for it follows that we cannot strictly regard a given change of height as equivalent to a corresponding change of latitude.

134. *Temperature of the Soil.*—The propagation of surface changes of temperature downwards into the ground takes place in the form of a wave whose amplitude decreases steadily till it ceases to be sensible ; the rate of propagation and of diminution of amplitude depending on the nature of the soil or rock and the extent of the surface fluctuations. It may be assumed generally that daily variations of temperature are insensible at depths greater than 3 to 5 feet, and annual variations 30 to 50 feet. Observations at Edinburgh and Greenwich have shown that at a depth of 25 feet the annual maximum and minimum occur about six months later than

---

[1] See Hann : *Handbuch der Klimatologie*, p. 146.

at the surface. The averages of ten years' observations at Eberswalde [1] at the surface, 6 inches, 1 foot, 2 feet, 3 feet, and 4 feet, show the normal distribution of temperature in the soil very clearly. In January, the temperature at the surface remains near the freezing point; at a depth of 4 feet a minimum of 35°·6 F. is reached about February 20th. The maximum at the surface (about 70° F.) occurs in the middle of July, and at 4 feet (about 61° F.) early in August. Temperature gradients are therefore very much steeper in summer when the surface is warmest than in winter when it is coldest. This series of observations, made in the open field, is of special value in showing in detail the manner in which the reversal of the gradients takes place, a subject rather beyond the scope of this book, and also from its association with a similar series made in a neighbouring pine forest. Comparison shows that in winter the soil of the forest is somewhat warmer than in the open field, the excess increasing with the depth; while in summer the difference is reversed, the forest soil being some 5° F. colder at the surface and 4 feet below it, and rather less at intermediate depths. The dates of maxima and minima are delayed some five to ten days at all depths. Similar conclusions with regard to the soil in the open have been reached by Buchan,[1] who shows from observations at several stations in Scotland the marked liability of loose sandy soils to excessive warming and intense frost, as compared with heavy clayey soils, on account of the smaller conducting power of the former. Buchan also obtains important results with regard to the effect of drainage on soil temperature. The mean annual temperature of arable land is, according to his observations, raised nearly 1° F. by

---

[1] Schubert, *Monats-u. Jahresmittel der Bodentemperaturen. Zeit. für Forst-u. Jagdwesen*, January, 1888.

[1] *Jour. Scot. Met. Soc.*, ii., p. 273. 1869.

drainage, and of hill pasture land nearly half that amount. Cold penetrates more readily into undrained soil, and less benefit is derived from high temperature through the loss of heat by evaporation. We have already seen that the effect of forest growth is to moderate the fluctuations of soil temperature, and the Scottish observations show that the same is true of all vegetable covering—a black surface of bare soil being a good radiator and absorber. These points are of great importance with reference to the change of temperature experienced by the roots of plants when they attain a growth sufficient to form a " braird " or covering ; as well as to their reaction on climate.

The modifying effect of exposure is, of course, considerable. Observations in the Innthal and Gschnitzthal near Innsbruck, discussed by F. von Kerner,[1] show that at a depth of about 1 foot, the warmest soil in summer is that having a S.E. exposure, but in winter S.W., and the coldest that having a northerly exposure, except in January and December, when the coldest exposure is east. The influence of exposure is most marked in spring and autumn, less so in summer and winter ; because the sun in its upward course attains nearly full power on a surface much inclined southward almost before it begins to be felt on one equally inclined to the north, and retains that power longer on its downward course. The following table, which gives the radiation received by surfaces inclined to N. and S. at an angle of 36°, expressed in percentages of what would be received if the rays fell perpendicular to them, will make this clear.

Height of Sun.	S. Exposure	N. Exposure.	Difference.
19° 27'	58·6	0·0	58·6
42° 55'	73·3	0·8	72·5
54° 39'	70·0	12·4	62·6
60° 23'	72·4	28·0	44·6

[1] *Sitzb. der Wiener Akad.*, May, 1891.

The fact that a S.E. exposure is the most favourable during summer is probably due to the increase of cloudiness towards afternoon. It is, of course, unsafe to draw general conclusions from a single series of observations like that just quoted, but it is important to note the *shortening* of the warm season as well as the diminished temperature in the case of a northern exposure.

135. *Moisture in the Soil.*—According to Wollny,[1] the effects of rainfall upon a soil—apart from loss by evaporation —are determined by (1) the surface drainage, (2) the vegetative covering, (3) the nature of the soil. In agricultural work the great object is to secure a dry or thoroughly porous surface soil, and at a proper depth, a permanent supply of moisture : the surface soil allows a supply of air to roots, and the soluble plant foods are not washed out, while the roots are encouraged to extend to a greater depth in search of moisture, increasing their supply of food and lessening the risks of damage from surface frost at the same time. The effect of a dry surface layer of soil in maintaining a supply of moisture in the sub-soil is well illustrated in the case of New South Wales, where in summer the surface of the ground is often baked hard and dry when the sub-soil is damp enough to keep weeds green and growing,[2] and its loss by evaporation is found to be almost *nil.*

The proportion of the rainfall which simply flows off the surface of the soil depends upon the inclination, the exposure—most with N., next W., E., and S.—the "closeness" of the surface, and the covering—most from bare land. The interception of water by vegetation increases with the

---

[1] *Untersuch. über das Verhalten der Niederschläge zur Pflanze und zum Boden. Forsch. auf dem Gebiete der Agrikulturphysik,* xii., 13, p. 316.

[2] H. C. Russell, *Rainfall Observations,* Sydney, 1886, p. 14.

density of the covering; cultivated land may receive as much as 31 per cent. less water when thickly covered than when bare.[1] We may therefore conclude that even with the same soil the quantity of water transmitted to any depth must be extremely variable. Other things being equal, it depends chiefly on the coarseness of the particles —the finer the grain of the soil, the greater difficulty the water has in penetrating; but we have also to take into account, apart from the rainfall, the water condensed directly from the atmosphere on the earth particles, which Giseler (*Berggeist*, 1878) has shown may amount to as much as 37 per cent. of the recorded rainfall; and again we must allow for the condition of the soil, for the same soil when dry will not transmit the same proportion of the water falling on it as when wet, and a frozen soil will not transmit water at all.

The net result of all these conditions, varying as they do from month to month, is well shown for the case of a heavy loam soil by the following averages of eleven years' observations at the experimental station at Rothamsted. These give the percentage of rainfall which reached a depth of 20 inches and 60 inches from a carefully weeded surface.

	20 inches per cent.	60 inches per cent.
Jan.	85	92
Feb.	86	81
Mar.	49	55
April	36	39
May	28	28
June	27	27
July	28	18
Aug.	32	28
Sept.	37	32

[1] Wollny, *loc. cit.*

					20 inches per cent.	60 inches per cent.
Oct.	.	.	.	.	60	54
Nov.	.	.	.	.	76	72
Dec.	.	.	.	.	80	79
Mar.—June	.	.	.		35	37
July—Sept.	.	.	.		32	26
Oct.—Feb.	.	.	.		76	76
Year	.	.	.	.	51	50

Ebermayer's [1] observations enable us to extend these results to different soils. The following means are based upon five years' observations of (1) coarse-grained quartz sand, (2) fine-grained ditto, (3) loose loam, (4) fine calcareous sand, (5) black peat, contained in pits nearly 4 feet deep.

PER CENT. OF RAINFALL PASSED.

Soil.	Year.	Winter.	Spring.	Summer.	Autumn.
1	86	100	74	84	85
2	107	129	96	104	104
3	94	125	98	77	98
4	48	66	30	39	51
5	39	56	37	34	38

Here the condensation in quartz sand, and even in loam, is very marked. Clay and humus allow little water to pass through; finely-divided humus, mixed with mineral earth, possesses greater absorbing power than pure peat, and therefore diminishes the amount of water transmitted with increase of humus through cultivation, and with cultivation of strong

[1] *Untersuch. uber die Sickerwassermengen in versch. Bodenarten Wollny's Forsch.* Bd. xiii.

transpiring plants the proportion also diminishes, an important fact in relation to the supply of springs.

136. *Effects of Climate on Plants.*—We have seen that the supply of water to the soil exercises an influence on vegetation chiefly through the selection and arrangement of plant food : and when that supply is provided by means of irrigation, plants grow and thrive quite as well as when it falls as rain. We are therefore justified in concluding that rainfall acts upon plants chiefly through the roots, and does not in general sensibly affect the parts above ground. On the other hand, we find that the temperature of the soil during the growing season is below that of the air, and are familiar with cases like that of the vine, which is often grown under glass at a high temperature, while the root is placed in ground fully exposed to the external air ; whence it appears that the temperature of the soil is not directly of first importance to the plant. It is possible, as A. de Candolle points out, that the soil may have some influence in modifying extremes of temperature through the supply of sap, especially in parts of the plant where, from the nature of the surface, conduction of heat and evaporation of moisture go on slowly. Thus, for example, the low temperature in the heart of the coco-nut is probably almost the same as that of the sap at the root. But it is obvious that for the most part temperature affects the growth of the plant above ground.

The inquiry, therefore, becomes much more complicated. For the word temperature as employed by the meteorologist means merely the temperature of the air in a shaded screen at a height of 4 feet above the ground ; while a plant rises from the ground, gradually increasing in height, and is exposed to great diversities of light and shade. Other considerations also come in, for we know that plants require light as well as heat, and cannot assume that they do not also require actinic rays. Plants require a supply of radiant energy to enable them to decompose carbonic acid and water in the leaf-cells, and it appears that the radiations most available to them for the purpose are of a special wave-length, or are arranged of special wave-lengths in certain proportions.

137. *Chemical Rays.*—To begin with rays of short wave-length. Sir William Siemens [1] has found that many species of plants grow freely and attain a full development of flower and fruit under the electric light, *provided* a screen of clear glass is interposed. On exposing the plants to the naked arc light they soon withered and shrivelled, but when the rays were filtered through glass a healthy growth was maintained. Now Stokes showed, in 1853, that rays from the electric arc are particularly rich in ultra-violet chemical rays, and that the greater part of these are intercepted by clear glass, *i.e.* that glass is opaque to them, just as it is opaque to the invisible heat rays from a source of lower temperature like a coal fire. Siemens therefore concluded that rays of short wave-length, when present in anything like excess, are not favourable but fatal to plant-growth. This result is again important in view of the absorption of blue rays by the atmosphere (§ 31), showing that the change of conditions experienced by plants at different elevations is not equivalent to that in different latitudes.

138. *Rays most Useful to Vegetation.*—Since, then, dark chemical rays are injurious to vegetation, and dark heat rays alone insufficient for proper growth, it follows that those most useful to plants generally are of intermediate wave-length—familiar to our eyes as yellow rays—precisely those in which the solar radiations are especially rich. While, therefore, we may artificially arrange such supplies of radiant energy as are necessary to plants by properly

[1] *B. A. Report*, 1881, p. 474.

combining dark and luminous rays (by means of heating apparatus, electric light, etc.) it appears that although the sun provides them in rays of all wave-lengths, it does so chiefly in those of a certain restricted period; and hence some measure of the total amount of energy required to produce a given physiological effect on a particular plant may be obtained from the intensity of these rays, taken as a measure of the whole solar radiations, and the length of time the plant is exposed to them. And since these " yellow " rays are the richest both in light and in heat, we may take either of these their effects as a measure of their intensity, and therefore of the total energy of the solar radiations under normal atmospheric conditions, *i.e.* so long as there is not special selective absorption of rays of particular wave-lengths. We assume that to whatever conclusions the physiological botanist may be led with reference to the relative action of heat and light upon vegetation for the particular case of the sun's rays, the *temperature, in so far as it depends on the action of these rays,* may be taken as at least a rough measure of the total effect, and proceed to inquire how far the air-temperature, as observed by a protected thermometer, is a measure of that temperature—this being for the present the most reliable datum available.

139. *Temperature of Plants.*—The direct determination of the actual external temperature of a plant as a whole at any given instant is obviously impossible. Every leaf, every part of the stem, every bud and petal, presents a different angle to the sun, and is protected to a different degree by other parts, or by neighbouring plants; consequently every part of the surface receives different amounts of heat. Again, every part of the structure has a different colour, so that each reflects and absorbs a different proportion of the rays falling upon it; and every part has a different structure—different conductivity for heat, and different supply of moisture to

modify the temperature by evaporation from the surface. The question is therefore forced into the form—How far do the variations of air temperature represent the variations experienced by the plant ? At first sight, it would seem that there should be a closer analogy between the experiences of *exposed* thermometers and of plants ; but we have already had to deal with the difficulties presented by radiation thermometers, and in addition to these there is the necessity of making some assumption that a particular kind of bulb resembles the average of the varied surface of vegetation. We have little reason to believe that a polished metal surface, or one of lamp black, is sensible to radiant heat in any manner resembling that of a leaf, even supposing that both were exposed in exactly the same way. On the other hand, we know that in most cases only a small proportion of the surface of any plant is at any one time exposed to direct sunlight, and that the parts most likely to have their temperature greatly raised by such exposure are just those most abundantly supplied with moisture, which by evaporation will reduce the temperature : considerations indicating a further approximation to "shade" conditions, at least so far as heat is concerned, although the same does not hold good for light, as will be seen immediately. But, as A. de Candolle[1] points out, plants themselves afford evidence which is almost conclusive ; for there is no observable difference between the north and south sides of a tree ; we do not gather flowers or fruit from the south side of a plant first and from the north later. We might therefore expect to find that, other things being equal, the average air temperature in shade would give an approximate measure of the average temperature of vegetation.

140. *Relation of Air Temperature to Insolation.*—But

---

[1] *Geographie botanique raisonnee*, p. 16.

here a difficulty comes in which it must be admitted greatly reduces the value of the method we are describing. Granting that the temperature of the air in some degree follows or represents that of vegetation as a whole, we cannot pretend that it is wholly dependent on the amount or intensity of insolation. While it is true that the temperature of the air is in the first place determined by the effect of the sun's rays on the surface of the ground, or on the vegetation covering it, that temperature is greatly modified by the motion of the air. When the prevailing winds at any place blow from a warmer region, the temperature of the air is undoubtedly higher than when they come from a colder, although the sun's heat may be the same; in the one case a certain amount of *transferred* temperature must be added, and in the other subtracted. Hence in the two cases the observed temperature of air and of vegetation bears a different and a varying relation to that of the sun's rays, and it ceases to be available as a measure of their intensity—that is of their light and heat.

The most important example of this which suggests itself is that of oceanic and insular climates. The sea acts as a kind of heating apparatus during winter and a refrigerator in summer, controlling the temperature independently of the direct insolation; and an ocean current may elevate or depress the temperature during the whole year. During the summer months the temperature is in general relatively lower, latitude for latitude, in an oceanic climate than in a continental, and while this is partly due to the direct decrease of the intensity of insolation through greater cloudiness, it is also partly on account of the coolness of the winds blowing in from the sea. The fact that the floras of the two climates are usually affected to such a degree by differences of rainfall that temperature considerations scarcely come in, may allow us to evade this difficulty in the more extreme cases, but, at the same time, makes it almost impossible to estimate its real importance.

The approximate heating effect on the air of a given amount of solar radiation has been calculated by Zenker,[1] who has found marked differences between observed and computed effects due to the transference of heat by currents and winds, but these results have not yet been applied to the questions we are discussing. Attempts to estimate solar intensity by means of air temperature must for the present be limited to regions where that temperature is chiefly regulated by the temperature of the earth's surface—that is, to continental climates.

141. *The Plant as a Heat Engine.*—Under this provision the various processes of germination, flowering, and maturation are then to be regarded as forming together a definite piece of work, requiring for its accomplishment the expenditure of a certain amount of energy ; and that energy, as supplied in the form of heat, to be transformed into what we may call vital energy by the plant, which becomes, from this point of view, a heat engine. Comparing the case of the plant with that of other heat engines, some further points of analogy suggest themselves, which may be taken as guides in defining our ideas. As a concrete example, suppose a steam-engine is employed to pump a given quantity of water out of a tank ; we may burn tons of coals and consume thousands of gallons of water in the boiler, but unless we raise a certain minimum pressure of steam, the engine refuses to move ; as soon as that minimum is reached, pumping begins, and the higher the pressure the faster the engine goes. The time taken to empty the tank is inversely as the rate of pumping : if the engine goes slow, it will take a long time—if faster, shorter ; but observe that whatever is done does not require to be done a second time. If

[1] *Met. Zeit.*, 1892, p. 336.

the pressure falls below the minimum again, the engine stops, but the work done is not lost, the water does not flow back into the tank. So with the plant; energy must be supplied at a certain pressure or intensity, or (since we have so agreed to measure it) at a certain temperature; until that minimum temperature is reached no growth takes place, and the more it is exceeded, the faster growth goes on; and all progress made is so much to the good—if the temperature falls below the minimum, growth stops, but there is no going back.

Now, suppose that (in the case of the steam-engine) the tank were altogether inaccessible, and that we had no means of ascertaining how much water it contained, or how far it had to be pumped, suppose that the only data to be obtained were hourly readings of the pressure gauge on the boiler, obviously it would be a hard task to calculate how much water the engine actually had to lift. But suppose that we require to pump the tank out once a year, and that each time all the machinery and gear are the same and in the same state of efficiency, then it would be not so difficult to compare, from the readings of the pressure gauge, the amount of water in the tank one year with the amount in another. We know that all the hours in which the pressure is below a certain point may be struck out, because the machinery must be at rest, and the rate of pumping at the other hours depends on the excess of the pressure above that point; so by adding the excess for each hour to the sum of all the previous hours since pumping began until the tank is empty, we evidently obtain a result representing the work done. Then if the machinery is the same every year, the variations in the sum will give some measure of the *differences* in the amount of water. But further, suppose after repeating this calculation a number of times we find that the pressure sum is the same every year, then we may fairly conclude that the quantity of water is always the same, and in this way arrive at an estimate of the work to be done each year ; knowing how much there is to do—the tale to be made up—we can each year calculate at any hour how far the work has progressed, and how much still remains to be done.

So with plants. Adding the excess above the minimum temperature required for growth for each hour from the time germination begins, we set a sum which measures the work done by the plant-engine, and we find year by year that between germination and maturation, whether the season be early or late, the sum remains nearly the same ; justifying our assumption that under favourable circumstances temperature, and *air* temperature, is a measure of the energy required for plant development, and that different progressive stages of that development correspond to definite amounts of work done. Hence at any point of the work we can, by looking up the temperature sum, ascertain how far the plant has progressed towards fruition, and how far it has still to go, and comparing that sum with the average of years for the same date, we get an accurate estimate of the earliness or lateness of the season, and the chances of full ripening before the supply of useful energy fails.

142. *Injurious Effects of Extremes of Temperature.*—Observe that for plant and steam-engine alike we have assumed the amount of power lost through machinery to be constant—the familiar case of dealing with one variable at a time. Such a condition corresponds most closely in the case of the plant to a state of perfect health, with proper supplies of normal food and moisture ; and hence we obtain a method of judging of these matters. For if the temperature account is satisfactory, and still a plant or crop seems backward in development, we may look for disease, and failing that, conclude that food supplies have run short; and so, by top-dressing or the like, save a crop before it is too late.

Again, we must carefully distinguish between the influence of temperature on the development of a healthy plant and its direct action upon plants themselves. All temperatures below a certain point are simply to be left out of consideration so far as positive growth is concerned, but this does not affect the fact that such low temperatures may kill the plant altogether. It was long believed that the fatal results of exposure to low temperatures were chiefly caused by destruction of plant tissue through the freezing of the contained water, but we know that while many plants are unable to withstand temperatures far above freezing, others are quite uninjured, although the sap in the tissues is frozen solid,[1] and it is now generally admitted that the action is physiological, arising from interference with the vital functions. A sudden change through a wide range of temperature is often almost as destructive as a severe frost. The following extracts from observations by Mr. E. J. Lowe, F.R.S.,[2] comparing the effects of the great frosts during the winters 1860-1 and 1878-9, afford interesting evidence that the destruction is not caused by the direct freezing of the sap. The greatest cold of 1860-1 exceeded that of 1878-9 by 10° F.; the minima were—6° F. in 1860-1, and + 4° F. in 1878-9. *See table opposite page.*

In the same way, when the temperature rises above a certain point, the rate of growth stops increasing either through destruction of tissue by excessive heat, or through simple exhaustion; just as the statement, that the steam-engine goes faster the greater the pressure, is not true when we

---

[1] See A. de Candolle, *loc. cit.* p., 33.

[2] *B. A. Report*, 1879, p. 377.

	1860-1.	1878-9.
Elm.	Uninjured.	Three-fourths of the boughs killed back at least two feet.
Bay (sweet).	Killed to the ground.	The ends of the shoots only killed, and all the leaves.
Fennel.	Uninjured.	All killed.
Roses, standards.	All killed.	Many killed, nearly all injured.
Laurel, Portugal.	Nearly all killed.	Uninjured.
Walnut.	Boughs killed, and one tree.	Uninjured except a want of vigour; leaves only half the usual size.

reach the point of bursting the boiler or straining all the rods and connections.

143. *Temperature at which Active Growth Begins.*—The first practical difficulty encountered in applying the considerations just explained to the growth of plants lies in determining the temperature at which active vegetation begins. The researches of Boussingault, to whom the method is originally due, and of A. de Candolle, who first made systematic application of it on a large scale, showed that in the case of most plants growing in North-Western Europe a temperature of 5° to 8° C. (41° to 46° F.) must be reached before signs of active growth are manifested; and although it cannot be said that the exact starting-point is accurately known for different species, subsequent investigations agree pretty unanimously in fixing it at 5°·5 or 6° C. The degree generally adopted in this country is 42° F. We

M

therefore assume, provisionally, that whenever the temperature rises above 42°, vegetation generally makes progress, and whenever it falls below that point, progress stops. It must certainly be admitted that in making this assumption we leave out of consideration what is, undoubtedly, a most important factor in practice. The warmth which suffices to make many plants germinate, and even flower, may be quite inadequate to make them produce fruit or to ripen that fruit. Buchan found that in Scotland wheat only ripens where the mean temperature during the summer months is as high as 56°·0 F.,[1] and that the chief difference between wheat and oat crops was not so much that the latter required a smaller total of heat to ripen it as that the former required greater concentration between the times of flowering and ripening. In warmer climates the excess above not only 42° but higher temperatures is in summer so continuous that this point might easily pass unnoticed, except for the inconsistencies introduced by it in the final sums of temperature ; but when we are dealing with a plant or crop anywhere near the limit of the area within which it can be cultivated, it becomes obvious that different stages of development require a different minimum before progress in them begins. All temperatures above 42° may supply sufficient " power " to enable the plant to form leaves and flowers, but that done the machinery may come to a stop unless a minimum of 50° or 56° is reached. Concerning this part of the subject little is as yet accurately known, and we must content ourselves for the present with the quite useful results derived from the assumption of the 42° minimum.

144. *Accumulated Temperature.*—The next difficulty is to find a satisfactory method of expressing the accumulated effect of a certain temperature, acting for a given time. Perfect accuracy would require a knowledge of the tempera-

[1] *Jour. Scot. Met. Soc.*, 1862, No. 2.

ture at every instant during the whole period; but, as we have seen in a former chapter, it is necessary to employ an indirect method which shall give, for any period, a close approximation to the *mean*. Hourly observations would give results very nearly correct, and we might express the accumulated temperature above 42° in hour degrees; subtracting 42° from the reading at each hour and adding all the positive differences together for the effective temperature, and the negative for the non-effective. But for most purposes it is sufficient, and it is always much more easy, to take the day as the unit—subtracting 42° from the mean of the day (calculated by methods already described)—and adding the differences, which give the required result expressed in *day*-degrees. The only serious error introduced by adopting so long an interval of time as twenty-four hours as a unit occurs where during one part of the day the temperature is not on the same side of 42° as the mean. This error, which affects all the work of the earlier investigators, is got rid of by the method of General Strachey already described (§ 94).

One other assumption involved in this manner of comparing temperature with effect upon growth must be recognised. We have taken for granted that the relation is of the most simple character; that the progress of the plant is simply proportional to the effective temperature and to the time. In this we are justified only by experience. Several investigators, notably Quetelet and Babinet, have thought to obtain better results by supposing the plant development to progress according to the square of the time or the effective temperature, but in this they have not been successful.

145. *Results obtained from Method of Accumulated Temperature.*—Having so far examined the ground, we may summarise our results in the proposition, that in order to the development and maturation of a healthy plant or crop,

besides proper supplies of food and moisture a certain amount of heat and light is necessary, which may be in continental climates measured in terms of accumulated temperature expressed to a first approximation as day degrees above a minimum of 42° F. That this rule, confessedly tentative and imperfect as it is, fairly represents the facts, appears from the following table extracted from a paper by Prof. J. H. Gilbert, F.R.S.[1]

Accumulated temperature in day degrees above 42° F., to date of harvest at Rothamsted Experimental Agricultural Station, calculated on the averages of observations in Eastern and Central England.

Year.				From date of frequent Weekly Excess. Degrees.				From return of Weekly Excess after interruption. Degrees.
1878	...	...	... ...	1999	...	...	... ...	1950
1879	...	...	... ...	1990	...	...	... ...	1961
1880	...	...	... ...	1976	...	...	... ...	1976
1881	...	...	... ...	1814	...	...	... ...	1804
1882	...	...	... ...	2026	...	...	... ...	1966
1883	...	...	... ...	1772	...	...	... ...	1645
1884	...	...	... ...	1847	...	...	... ...	1686
1885	...	...	... ...	1774	...	...	... ...	1696
Highest	...	...	...	2026	...	...	... ...	1976
Lowest	...	...	... ...	1772	...	...	... ...	1645
Mean	...	...	... ...	1900	...	...	... ...	1836

Calculating from Greenwich observations by the less accurate method of multiplying the monthly means of temperature by the number of days from 1st April to date of harvest, Gilbert finds the average for the 27 years 1852 to 1878 to

---

[1] *Archives des Sciences physiques et naturelles*, Geneva, 1886, p. 421.

amount to 1980°, the highest being 2183° and the lowest 1809°. These figures are necessarily too large, but making allowance for error, are in fair agreement with those in the table ; and we may take it that for wheat the accumulated temperature required is about 1900° F. Hervé-Mangon, employing daily means, obtained a result corresponding to 1854° for north-eastern France from eight years observations. M. E. Risler gives 2192° for Nyon, in Switzerland. For spring-sown barley, Boussingault gives 2005°, De Candolle about 2100°, and Hervé-Mangon, 1989°; from which, as Gilbert further points out, it would seem that the totals required for wheat and for at least the finer kinds of barley are nearly the same.

The figures quoted have been derived almost exclusively from stations at which the climates are for the most part continental in character. The data available for discussion by this method are as yet too meagre to merit extensive treatment, and it is impossible to trace with any accuracy the relation of the solar energy received by plants to the observed temperature in shade in different climates. A. de Candolle found that in latitude 56° N., Alyssum required 50° to 70° more in Scotland than in Sweden, and Spindletree about 200° more ; Columbine 900° more in Scotland than in Eastern Russia. In latitude 57° 30′ to 58° the Alder buckthorn required 350° less at Viatka than in Scotland, and in latitude 59° the flax-seed (*Radiola binoides*) 45° less in Sweden than in Orkney.[1] All these facts may be taken as showing that the accumulated temperature is not the same measure of solar energy in the different localities, but that Scotland is as it were artificially warmed by the sea.

146. *Conditions under which the Method is Applicable.*— In view of all the evidence, we may fairly conclude that in

[1] *Geographie botanique raisonnée*, p. 402.

continental climates, where the temperature of the lower strata of the atmosphere is chiefly controlled by terrestrial radiation, air temperature fairly represents the intensity of the sun's action ; but that in oceanic climates the balance of light and heat is disturbed, and a certain proportion of the latter must, when positive, be treated separately like the warmth of a hot-house. This extra allowance of "dark heat" is, of course, beneficial just as the warming of the hot-house is, as is obvious from the fact that spring flowers bloom about a month earlier in the west and south of England and Ireland than in the midland counties and Scotland,[1] but its influence is probably different from that of sun heat which would alone produce the same average temperature. When the effect is negative, as it generally is during the warmer months of the year, the deficiency reduces the apparent power of the sun's rays as shown by air temperature, and the relation between heat and light is altered in the opposite direction.

147. *Influence of Rainfall.*—Important as these considerations undoubtedly are in any scientific treatment of the relations of climate to plant-growth, it is probable that they do not very seriously affect the value of the method of accumulated temperatures in its application to practical agriculture, because in those climates where the air temperature is greatly modified by the influence of the sea, the excessive humidity and rainfall usually preclude the cultivation of any but the coarser kinds of cereals. Buchan finds that "where the mean summer temperature is as low as 56°·0, the cultivation of wheat is quite possible even though the character of the springs be cold and backward, *provided always* that the rainfall in summer and autumn be not in excess," and again that temperature conditions on the west

[1] See Hoffmann : *Pflanzen-phänologischen Beobachtungen in Europa.* Giessen, 1885.

coast of Scotland are in many places more favourable than on the east, but " on account of the moist atmosphere the crops run rapidly into straw, which being weak from a deficiency of silica are more easily laid by the torrents of rain and violent winds."[1] Hence it appears that the difficulty lies not in supplying power to the engine but in keeping it in working order.

So long as the required total of sun heat and light can be made up the more uniform a climate is the better, for vegetation is specially liable to injury from sudden large changes of temperature during the period of active growth. In the south of England, where the mean summer temperature is $4°·0$ F. above the critical point required for wheat, the damage and loss in a bad year is usually more complete than in the more equable climate of the wheat-growing districts of Scotland, where the usual margin is only $2°$ F., and even that is eked out by the greater length of the days.[2]

148. *Effect of Vegetation on Climate: Forests.*—The modifications of climate produced by the covering of vegetation on the surface of the ground have already been noticed, and their nature will be sufficiently intelligible from the foregoing details of the reverse problem. As an extreme case we may take the differences observed between the climates of open country and of forest-land under similar conditions. Other things being equal, the range of temperature is smaller in the former than in the latter. The daily minima of temperature are higher, and the daily maxima lower in the forest than in the open, much as we find on comparing sea with land. During still summer weather a movement of the air exactly analogous to land and sea breezes is sometimes observed on the outskirts of a forest, most frequently in the evening, for the lowering of the maxima is in general much

[1] *Jour. Scot. Met. Soc.,* 1862.
[2] *Jour. Scot. Met. Soc.,* 1863., i., p. 15

more marked than the raising of the minima. The amount by which the range is decreased depends greatly on the thickness of the growth, and on the species of tree constituting the forest. It is in the case of evergreen trees least in midwinter, increases steadily till August and then again decreases. In the case of deciduous trees the difference is least in April just before the leaves come out, increases rapidly for two months, attains its maximum in July, and after September diminishes rapidly on the falling of the leaves. During summer, at least, the daily maximum is somewhat later and the daily minimum somewhat earlier in forest than in field. The observations of the German Forestry department,[1] upon which these results are based, afford the further important fact that the variations of temperature among the upper branches of forest trees are intermediate between those near the ground and in the open, but tend to follow the former more closely.

According to Eckert,[2] the amount of vapour (absolute humidity) decreases from the ground upwards amongst trees if the soil be wet, but increases after a continuance of dry weather, the supply of moisture to the leaves by transpiration holding out longer than that to the surface of the soil. Compared with open country the absolute humidity is usually greater not only amongst the trees but above them ; and the same is true of the relative humidity : but in these cases it is impossible to lay down a general rule, as the conditions are chiefly determined by the distribution of rainfall and the nature of the soil and vegetation in the open.

That forests have, in certain cases, a marked influence upon rainfall has been well established by Blanford in India and by Müttrich and Ebermayer in Germany. By comparing a region in the Central Provinces, planted in 1875,

[1] See Müttrich, *Met. Zeit.*, 1891, p. 55.
[2] *Met. Zeit.*, 1890, p. 361.

with surrounding districts, Blanford found that the rainfall steadily increased year by year with the growth of the young trees.[1] A similar method, although applied on a smaller scale, gave identical results in the heart of the Luneburger Haide.[2]

[1] *Jour. Asiatic Soc. of Bengal*, i., 1887.
[2] Müttrich, *Met. Zeit*, 1892, p. 307.

INDEX.

A